PHYSICS OF STEREO/QUAD SOUND

PHYSICS OF STEREO/QUAD SOUND

JOSEPH G. TRAYLOR

Iowa State University Press / Ames

DEDICATED TO Joan, my wife, and Joy Gayle, our preschooler

Two persons full of music

JOSEPH G. TRAYLOR, assistant professor of physics at Buena Vista College in Storm Lake, Iowa, holds the Ph.D. degree in physics from the University of Tennessee. His previous experience includes teaching in the field of musical acoustics at Iowa State University and research in solid state physics.

TK
7881.8
T73

© 1977 The Iowa State University Press
Ames, Iowa 50010. All rights reserved

Composed and printed by The Iowa State University Press

First edition, 1977

Library of Congress Cataloging in Publication Data

Traylor, Joseph G   1942–
  Physics of stereo/quad sound.

    Bibliography: p.
    Includes index.
    1. Sound—Recording and reproducing.
2. Stereophonic sound systems.   I. Title.
TK7881.8.T73   621.389'33   77-21768
ISBN 0-8138-0025-0

CONTENTS

PREFACE

If you are interested in buying sound reproduction equipment, you ask yourself a hundred times, "Is this the right loudspeaker for me?" or, "Is the salesman really advising in *my* best interest? Many people find themselves confused in the stereo buying market. They are not sure what parts of a system are most important or what are the most appropriate ways for judging performance of equipment or comparing specifications. When they shop they are confused by the fact that either "they all sound good" or "the most expensive one made the others sound terrible." Most buyers feel that if they knew a little more about the subject of sound reproduction, they would be wiser consumers. I agree.

I have written this book for two reasons: to help people understand basic principles of audio and to attract students, who would not otherwise do so, to think about basic principles of physics. Audio is important to me; by that I mean that to me audio is an exciting adventure. Whether sitting before loudspeakers listening to a Bach fugue, scrubbing the kitchen floor with the background support of a Telemann concerto, or trying to mix and master the taping of a choir performance, both the quality of the reproduction and the music itself are challenging and stimulating. For me, part of this appreciation comes from knowing how it works. It is the appreciation for sound reproduction that I wish to share and encourage.

Physics is important to me. That is, I believe that a person can learn a great deal about nature by studying physics and can become a broader person because of it. However, not very many people *want* to learn physics enough to study it by itself. To study physics while digging into some other topic that already interests us is much more fun. If we can learn physical principles (which apply to all of nature) while examining, say, how to put four different sound signals into one groove of a record, all the better.

This book contains information about both audio and physics. The audio coverage touches enough topics in sound reproduction to give the reader a grasp of the "how's" and "why's" of the equipment. A glossary is included to assist those with nontechnical backgrounds.

The physics coverage provides a rather broad introductory survey for nonscientists. Most topics of classical physics and a few, selected topics of modern physics are included. The approach is to present physical principles to explain aspects of sound reproduction. A section on mechanics, not required for sound reproduction treatment, is included in Appendix 1 for completeness.

In this book we are treating the *reproduction* of sound rather than its production (acoustics); and although some topics are common to each field, most material in this book is not included in texts on musical acoustics. Furthermore, acoustics is not prerequisite to this treatment, although persons with acoustics experience may more fully appreciate some topics here. For any persons interested, excellent books on musical acoustics are suggested in the reading list.

I have tried to maintain a low mathematical level for the purpose of reaching students of all backgrounds. I have stated and used equations if the principles are better illustrated by numbers describing the sizes of the quantities involved. For example, if someone says the number of atoms in the period at the end of this sentence is "lots of atoms," it means nothing. Even "millions of atoms" doesn't help us appreciate the number. If someone says "10^{18} (1,000,000,000,000,000,000) atoms," then we begin to gain perspective. Physics, basically a quantitative science, loses something without numbers. Questions and exercises are included with each chapter to assist in appreciation of the physics.

I express thanks for the patience and skill of the secretarial staff, the drafting professionals who developed my sketches, physics colleagues who offered encouragement, and the many students who used these notes and gave suggestions. Several publishers allowed reproduction of their material, RCA provided photographs, and Shure Brothers, Inc., supplied original slides for reproduction.

It is my hope that this work will be as beneficial to the reader as the preparation of it has been to me.

PHYSICS OF STEREO/QUAD SOUND

1
FUNDAMENTALS OF SOUND: BASIC PHYSICAL LAWS

1.1 HOW SOUND WAVES CARRY ENERGY

We define a sound wave to be motion of atoms or molecules such that all particles in a small region of space oscillate in the line of travel of the wave. For example, consider a sound wave in air. Figure 1.1A shows the undisturbed air molecules at some time before the sound wave passes. The positions of the particles are entirely random. In fact, if we consider a volume of air that is much larger than the volume of one molecule (a cubic centimeter would be about 10^{24} times larger than a molecule!), the average positions of the molecules are equally spaced, as indicated in Fig. 1.1A.

When a sound wave passes, the positions of the particles are disturbed as illustrated in Fig. 1.1B. Note regions of high density in which the molecules are closely packed. These regions have a local air pressure higher than the atmospheric pressure at that instant. Other regions are rarified and have both lower density and lower pressure than the surrounding undisturbed air. Thus when the wave passes through the air, some molecules are displaced from their initial positions into regions of high density, leaving the initial position in a rarified or low density state.

Later the molecules return to their initial position, since the high density region has a higher pressure than the neighboring low density

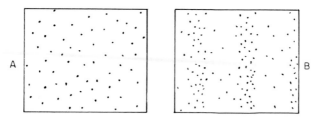

Fig. 1.1. Schematic representations of positions of molecules in a gas. A: Random arrangement when gas is in equilibrium. B: Arrangement as sound wave passes through gas.

region and the particles are pushed away. In fact, the molecules will not stop at their initial position but will overshoot, creating new regions of higher density.

Let us forget individual molecules for a moment and note that the region of high pressure actually moves through space as a unit! This region could be called a wave front. If this wave front finally approached the diaphragm of an ear or of a microphone, the high pressure region would push in on the diaphragm and cause it to move inward. As the region of high pressure passed by, the region of low pressure would reach the diaphragm. Then the higher pressure would be behind the diaphragm and lower pressure in front, and the diaphragm would move outward. The result is that the diaphragm would oscillate just as the air molecules do.

1.2 PROPERTIES OF WAVES

Consider the wave again. In Fig. 1.2 we use two different ways to represent the pressure of the air in a region containing a sound wave. Although the picture of the actual positions of the particles as shown in Fig. 1.2A may be simpler to visualize, the conceptual plot of Fig. 1.2B is more convenient for study. The high points on Fig. 1.2B identify regions in which the pressure is a maximum, somewhat above the average pressure of the surrounding air, p_{atm} (atmospheric pressure). The low points identify regions in which the pressure is below atmospheric pressure.

The wave plotted in Fig. 1.2B is called a *sine* wave and such a pressure variation is said to be a *sinusoidal* variation. Consider the characteristics of such a wave, as shown in Fig. 1.3. The *amplitude* of the wave is denoted by A and indicates the maximum deviation from the

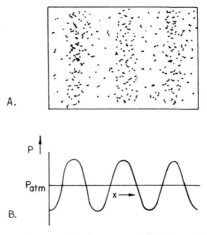

A.

B.

Fig. 1.2. A: Positions of gas molecules as sound wave passes. B: Graphic representation of pressure in gas; horizontal line represents initial, undisturbed pressure (P_{atm} = atmospheric pressure).

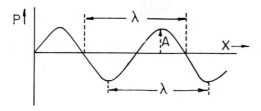

Fig. 1.3.   Plot of pressure versus position in air sample.

reference line. Note that for this sine wave the maximum negative deviation (below the reference line) is also equal to A. Since the figure
represents pressure on the vertical axis, A corresponds to the maximum
deviation in pressure above and below atmospheric pressure.

The symbol λ is used to denote *wavelength*. The wavelength is the
distance between neighboring points on the wave that have identical
characteristics. For example, the distance between two adjacent maxi-
mums or two adjacent minimums is one wavelength. The wavelength
is a very useful quantity. For example, in most materials the speed of
travel of a sound wave is the same for all audible sound waves. If we
know the wavelength λ and the velocity v of the wave, we can find the
frequency f by the wave relation

$$f = v/\lambda \tag{1.1}$$

or as it is normally written

$$v = f\lambda \tag{1.2}$$

As an example, the speed of sound in air at room temperature is
about 345 m/s, so if the sound has a wavelength of 0.785 m, the frequency must be

$$f = \frac{v}{\lambda} = \frac{345 \text{ m/s}}{0.785 \text{ m}} = 440 \frac{c}{s} = 440 \text{ Hz}$$

which is the musical note, concert A. The symbol Hz stands for hertz,
named in honor of a pioneer in the study of waves, Heinrich Hertz. Note
that from this example we know quite a bit about the motion of particles
in a sound wave. We know that (1) the wave itself moves through the
air at 345 m/s, (2) the motion of the air at $(x + 0.785)$ m is exactly the
same as the motion of the air at x m, and (3) the individual air molecules
are oscillating at 440 c/s.

Before continuing, we should consider two principal types of waves:
longitudinal—the motion of an individual particle is along the direction
of travel of the wave, and *transverse*—the individual particle moves perpendicular to the direction of travel of the wave. (*Water waves* are a
third kind; the motion of a water molecule is a complicated rotary motion. We will not be concerned with this type.) Figure 1.4 shows longitudinal and transverse waves along a one-dimensional medium. Sound

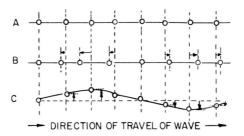

Fig. 1.4. A: Undisturbed medium. B: Longitudinal wave. C: Transverse wave. Small arrows show displacement of particles at instant waves pass by.

waves travel in air as longitudinal waves. Later we shall study radio waves, which propagate as transverse waves.

1.3 STANDING WAVES

A very useful phenomenon of waves is *standing waves,* which result from the summation of two waves of the same frequency traveling in opposite directions in the same medium. For example, if a violin string is plucked, the pluck bump travels along the string in both directions away from the point of initial disturbance. Both waves reach their respective ends of the string, and since the ends are fixed and cannot move, the waves are reflected. They then travel along the string approaching each other, pass each other, and eventually again reflect, etc. The process is illustrated in Fig. 1.5. (1) The initial pluck can be visualized as being composed of two bumps (dashed lines) half as high as the actual pluck, which travel in opposite directions on the string. (2) The two bumps move. The resulting displacement is everywhere equal to the sum or superposition of the two bumps. (3) The bumps near the ends of the string. Note that the total displacement of the string is nearly zero. (4) The bumps reflect from the ends. Note that the bumps are reversed in displacement from positive to negative, but the amplitudes are unchanged. Also, the direction of travel of the bumps has reversed. (5) As the bumps approach each other the displacement of the string approaches a peaked shape. (6) When the bumps pass one another, the string displays its maximum negative displacement. (7) The bumps continue, and the pattern repeats itself. (8) The net motion of the string is a smooth up-and-down oscillation. The solid line represents the displacement of the string at one time, and the dashed line at a later time.

Figure 1.6 shows another transverse standing wave pattern on a string. Note the positions on the string, called *nodes,* where no displacement occurs. The ends of the string are nodes since the ends are tied down and not allowed to vibrate. Other positions on the string may have some displacement. The positions showing the maximum amount of vibration are called *antinodes.*

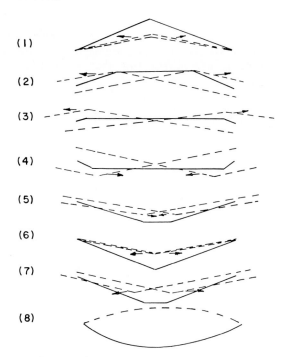

Fig. 1.5. Process of generating standing waves on string.

In this study, our interest with standing waves is related primarily to the phenomenon termed *resonance*. Only certain waves can cause standing waves on the above string, because only certain waves have the appropriate wavelength to "just fit" between the fixed ends of the string (that is, the ends of the string must be nodes). Therefore, only certain waves will excite the string, causing it to vibrate in a standing wave pattern. The response of the string to these particular frequencies is resonance. This resonance phenomenon is responsible for the proverbial operatic soprano's breaking of crystal glass, for the very large motion of a child's playground swing when only small pushes are applied, and for the necessity for marching army columns to break cadence when crossing bridges.

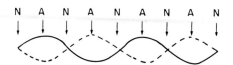

Fig. 1.6. String vibrating in standing wave pattern with five nodes (labeled N) and four antinodes (labeled A). Solid line represents position of string at one time, and dotted line represents string at later time.

Most people have experienced resonance for longitudinal sound waves in air when singing in the shower. As one sings different notes, some notes appear much louder than others because the shower stall resonates certain frequencies, indicating that a standing wave pattern has been created in the air of the "acoustical chamber" of the shower.

Consider the nodal pattern for standing longitudinal sound waves in air in a chamber. Where are the nodes? That question is meaningful only when we identify the kind of wave pattern we are describing. For example, air molecules at the walls cannot move (cannot penetrate the wall); thus, walls are nodes if we are describing displacement waves showing the vibration of the actual air molecules. However, walls are antinodes if we are describing the pressure in the air, since the molecules accumulate at the wall and create a large pressure. One such pattern is illustrated in Fig. 1.7.

The study of resonances in air columns and on vibrating strings leads one into the interesting field of musical instruments. For example, vibrating strings can have only particular frequencies because the ends of the strings are clamped down and therefore must be nodal positions. Thus, only standing waves of certain wavelengths can exist on the string. As a string player clamps a string down with a finger, the effective vibrating length of the string (and therefore the frequency) changes. Brass instruments have resonant air columns for producing sounds. By changing the lengths of the air columns with slides as in trombones or valved pathways as in trumpets or tubas, the player changes the pitch of the instrument. Woodwind players change pitch by opening holes and therefore modifying the effective length of the instrument. This

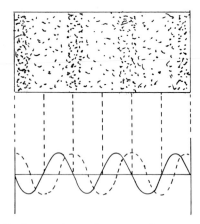

Fig. 1.7. Positions, displacements, and pressure in wave. Upper part of drawing shows positions of air molecules at an instant due to longitudinal standing wave in chamber. Lower part shows plot of displacement (solid line) of molecules indicating nodes at walls. Plot of pressure (dashed line) shows antinodes at walls.

rich subject may be explored thoroughly in the works by Benade and Backus given in the reading list at the end of this book.

Here, we are interested in resonance because of its effects in sound reproduction, such as the response of a stylus vibrating in a record groove or the standing wave pattern of sound inside a loudspeaker enclosure.

1.4 FORCE

We have investigated the nature of sound waves in air. Consider the effect that the wave may have on some object such as a diaphragm of a microphone. Of course, we know the answer: because the sound wave creates a difference in air pressure between the front and back sides, the diaphragm experiences a net *force*. It is this concept of force that we now discuss.

Force is so common in our daily experience that we seldom think about it. We are aware that the Earth is held in orbit around the sun by a gravitational force, one electrically charged particle can repel or attract another by an electrical force, magnets can attract bits of iron by a magnetic force, and some objects tend to resist sliding because of frictional forces. Our intent here is not to investigate why these forces exist but rather what is the result of applying a force.

For example, suppose we place a matchbox and a large book on a smooth surface such as fresh ice at a skating rink. Then we gently strike the two objects one at a time with approximately the same impact so that they slide across the surface. The matchbox briskly slides across the ice, but the book moves very slowly. Why are the results so different if both objects experience the same force? The answer depends on two quantities that we now introduce, mass and acceleration.

Mass is the property of a body that causes it to resist a change in its motion. Mass has been called the "inertia" of a body and some describe it as the "amount of material" in a body. The matchbox has very little mass and thus does not resist changes of motion. It responds to our striking it by rapidly sliding across the smooth surface. The book on the other hand has large mass and and a great resistance to a change in motion.

The second quantity, *acceleration,* is not so new to us. Acceleration is how fast we change velocity. An object moving at a constant speed of 5 meters per second (m/s) has no acceleration. An object whose speed is changing such that its speed increases by 1 m/s each second is accelerating. Its acceleration is given by

$$\text{acceleration} = \frac{\text{change of speed}}{\text{change of time}} = 1 \frac{\text{m/s}}{1 \text{ s}} = 1 \frac{\text{m}}{\text{s}^2}$$

This quantity may be read as "one meter per second per second" or "one meter per second squared." When an object's speed is decreasing, it is said to have a negative acceleration.

Force F is the product of mass m and acceleration a. This important result, called Newton's second law of motion, may be written

$$F = ma \tag{1.3}$$

Remembering our matchbox and book, we see that if we apply the same force to each, we shall have quite different accelerations due to the very different masses of the two objects:

$$F_{\text{box}} = F_{\text{book}}$$

$$m_{\text{box}}\, a_{\text{box}} = m_{\text{book}}\, a_{\text{book}}$$

$$a_{\text{box}} = \frac{m_{\text{book}}}{m_{\text{box}}}\, a_{\text{book}}$$

Therefore, if the mass of the book is 1000 times greater than the mass of the box, then the acceleration of the box will be 1000 times greater than the acceleration of the book.

The study of forces and accelerations is a discipline of physics called mechanics. If we know the acceleration of a body, we can predict the future motion of the body: where it will be, when it will get there, etc. We have included in Appendix 1 a brief treatment of mechanics. Those who are interested will find that discussion helpful in understanding motion.

In this study of sound reproduction we use the concept of force more often than the equations describing force. One force, however, merits special attention for this study: the force that a particle experiences when it is attached to the end of a spring. Consider Fig. 1.8. If left undisturbed, the particle hangs at some rest position called the *equilibrium* position. Suppose we pull the particle down a small distance (thereby stretching the spring) to the position marked in the figure as the minimum vertical position. We hold it there and then release it. The particle will oscillate about its equilibrium position. Note that its

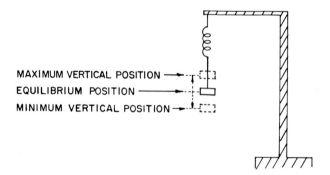

MAXIMUM VERTICAL POSITION

EQUILIBRIUM POSITION

MINIMUM VERTICAL POSITION

Fig. 1.8.   Motion of mass hanging from spring; mass oscillates above and below its equilibrium position.

maximum vertical position is just as far above equilibrium as the minimum position is below equilibrium. This deviation of position away
from equilibrium is called displacement, and the maximum displacement
is called amplitude just as in the description of waves in the previous
sections. In fact, this oscillating particle motion is itself a type of periodic wave motion. If a pen were attached to the particle, and the pen
were touching a moving chart as shown in Fig. 1.9, the resulting pattern would be the same as the wave pattern we have previously discussed.

1.4.1 Hooke's Law and Simple Harmonic Motion

The spring force discussed in the previous paragraph occurs in so
many areas of sound reproduction that we shall give it special consideration. This force is the restoring force on an object when the particle
is moved away from its rest position. The springs in Figs. 1.8 and 1.9
are examples, and the resulting motion for each is oscillatory.

Consider the force that the spring exerts on the particle. The force
may be described by an equation called Hooke's law:

$$F = -kx \tag{1.4}$$

where k is the spring constant (large k means a strong spring, small k
means a weak spring), and x is the displacement of the object away from
its equilibrium position. The minus sign means that the force on the
object is always oppositely directed to the displacement. If we pull the
object up, the restoring force is downward; if we pull it down, the restoring force is upward. Thus, the restoring force always tries to restore
the particle to the equilibrium position. At the equilibrium position
there is no force on the object.

Hooke's law describes a *linear* force. That is, if we pull the object
down 1 cm, we get some particular amount of restoring force from the
spring. If we pull it down 2 cm, we get exactly twice that amount of

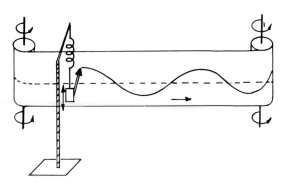

Fig. 1.9.   Up-and-down oscillations of particle on spring are recorded on moving chart as wave.

force. However, some amount of stretch of the spring is finally reached beyond which it no longer behaves linearly and the system will no longer obey Hooke's law. Hooke's law is usually valid only for small displacements of a system.

We begin to see how this discussion applies to our study of sound reproduction. The diaphragm in a microphone is connected to the case of the microphone by some type of stiff material. This mounting is called a suspension, and as the diaphragm moves in and out, controlled by the air pressure variations in a sound wave, this suspension flexes as does a spring. For small motions of the diaphragm, the suspension puts a restoring force on the diaphragm as described by Hooke's law. If the sound wave has sinusoidal pressure variations, the diaphragm will follow with sinusoidal displacements. However, if the pressure wave has such large amplitude that it drives the diaphragm far from its equilibrium position and the suspension ceases to obey Hooke's law, then the diaphragm will exhibit motion that is different from the pressure variations of the sound wave. The output signal of the microphone will then be different from the input signal. Such behavior is called *nonlinear,* and the result is distortion in the output of the microphone.

Finally, note that any spring force system that obeys Hooke's law will vibrate with a motion called *simple harmonic motion.* A system that exhibits simple harmonic motion has a resonant frequency, a natural mode of oscillation, that is characteristic of the system. We will not go into the mathematics to calculate that frequency but will give the result for a simple spring:

$$f = \frac{1}{2\pi}\sqrt{\frac{k}{m}} \tag{1.5}$$

From this equation we know that the resonant frequency tends to be higher for very strong springs and tends to be lower when the object being moved is very massive. (Later we discuss the effect of the resonance in the diaphragm-suspension system on a microphone's response.)

Note that the resonant frequency does not depend on the amplitude of the motion of the object. As long as the displacement of the particle is small enough that Hooke's law is obeyed, the frequency is independent of whether the motion of the particle is small or large.

1.5 ENERGY, INTENSITY, AND POWER

We have seen that a sound wave can exert a force on an object such as a diaphragm. Another way to think of this effect is to say that the sound wave can transmit energy from a source to a device such as a diaphragm. In physics, *energy* means the ability to do work, that is, to move something such as a diaphragm or eardrum. We eat food to give us chemical energy to be able to move ourselves throughout the day. We use sunshine to give water molecules enough energy to move out of clothing drying on a clothesline and to move electrons in our skin to cause the chemical changes known as tanning. We burn natural gas to get heat energy to move electrons to cause the chemical changes known as cooking. We use electrical energy to turn motors, to perk coffee, and to create artificial illumination. A brief treatment of mechanical energy is given in Appendix 1.

Although the formulas may be cumbersome, it is useful to know the amount of energy transferred by a wave. The relation is

$$\text{energy per unit volume} = 2\pi^2 f^2 A^2 \rho \tag{1.6}$$

where: f = frequency
     A = amplitude
     ρ = density of medium in which wave is traveling; that is, amount of material (mass) in unit volume

"Energy per unit volume" refers to the amount of energy transmitted in some certain volume of gas, such as one cubic meter.

The interesting consequences of Eq. (1.6) that concern us are the comparison of the energies of two waves of different frequencies or different amplitudes. For example, consider the effect on the diaphragm of a microphone from a 100-Hz signal and from a 1000-Hz signal of the same amplitude, both traveling in air. Thus,

$$\frac{\text{energy of 1000-Hz signal}}{\text{energy of 100-Hz signal}} = \frac{2\pi^2 \ (1000 \ \text{Hz})^2 \ A^2 \ \rho}{2\pi^2 \ (100 \ \text{Hz})^2 \ A^2 \ \rho}$$

$$= \frac{1,000,000}{10,000} = 100$$

showing that the 1000-Hz signal would impart 100 times as much energy to the microphone as the 100-Hz signal of equal amplitude.

A quantity of more direct interest to us than energy in a wave is the *intensity* of the wave. This quantity refers to the amount of energy transmitted across a given area in a certain amount of time. If some amount of energy falls on the area of an eardrum in one hour, say, the wave may not be very intense. However, if the same energy fell on the eardrum in one second, the wave may be described as very intense. The formula for intensity I is

$$\text{intensity} = \frac{\text{energy}}{\text{area} \times \text{time}} = 2\pi^2 f^2 A^2 \rho v \tag{1.7}$$

where v is the speed of travel of the wave. Note that intensity has the same dependence on frequency and amplitude as does energy per unit volume.

Finally, the quantity power should be discussed. We have all heard of power, whether it be in relation to automobile engines or amplifiers.

Power refers to how fast energy is delivered from some source. Both an economy car and a racing car can go 50 mi/hr, but the racing car can attain that speed starting from rest much sooner. Why? Because its engine has more power; that is, it can deliver energy faster. For a traveling sound wave,

$$\text{power} = \frac{\text{energy}}{\text{time}} = \text{intensity} \times \text{area}$$

$$\text{intensity} = \text{power}/\text{area}$$

Thus, for a constant-area diaphragm such as an eardrum, a wave delivered from a source of high power will have greater intensity than a wave from a source of low power. In the physics of music it is recognized that the loudness of a sound is related to the intensity of the sound wave. The relation is complicated and depends on human aural and psychological response. For example, two persons may agree that two sounds are equally loud, but they seldom agree that one sound is twice as loud as another. However, they do agree that when the intensity of a sound is increased, the loudness also increases. Note that loudness is a psychological response and therefore is not a measurable physical quantity. In this book we wish to employ only measurable quantities; thus, we shall use intensity or power instead of loudness.

1.6 DECIBEL

Intensity levels may be described conveniently in decibels (dB). Consider the intensity range of normal human hearing. First we measure the intensity of the softest sound we can hear: the minimum perceptible intensity. Then we measure the intensity of the loudest sound that does not damage our ears: the threshold of pain. Comparing the two measurements, we find the maximum intensity to be 1,000,000,000,000 times higher than the minimum! The range is so wide that conventional counting numbers such as a million million become awkward and inconvenient for intensity comparisons. For a more convenient scale, we use the logarithm. Recall that the logarithm of a number is defined by

$$\log x = y \quad \text{for} \quad x = 10^y \tag{1.8}$$

That is, the logarithm of 100 is 2 since $10^2 = 100$, and $\log 20,000 = 4.3$ since $10^{4.3} = 20,000$. Note that the logarithm of 1,000,000,000,000 is 12 since $10^{12} = 1,000,000,000,000$.

The range of intensities perceived by normal hearing could be expressed as numbers between 0 and 12 by using the logarithms. When used for intensity ratios, these logarithms are called bels. Normally, however, we use the *decibel* (dB) scale defined by

$$\text{difference in intensity level, dB} = 10 \log \frac{I_2}{I_1} \tag{1.9}$$

The difference in intensity levels between the minimum and maximum intensities of normal hearing is then

$$10 \log \frac{I_{max}}{I_{min}} = 10 \log 1,000,000,000,000$$

$$= 10 \log 10^{12} = 10(12) = 120 \text{ dB}$$

We have defined the difference of levels by Eq. (1.9). We may also define an absolute scale by denoting the minimum perceptible sound level 0 dB and comparing all other sounds with it. (The accepted standard is an intensity of 10^{-12} W/m² for 0 dB. Table 1.1. shows the dB ratings of various sounds.

The dB scale is convenient for comparison of other types of large numbers. For example, the voltage output of an amplifier may be a million times greater than the voltage of the input. The same holds for current. However, one must remember that the dB concept is reserved for power or intensity comparisons. It is useful for voltage V since power is proportional to the square of voltage. Thus, Eq. (1.9) becomes

$$\text{difference in intensity level, dB} = 10 \log \frac{I_2}{I_1} = 10 \log \frac{P_2}{P_1}$$

$$= 10 \log \frac{V_2^2}{V_1^2} = 10 \log \left(\frac{V_2}{V_1} \right)^2 = 20 \log \left(\frac{V_2}{V_1} \right) \qquad (1.10)$$

If the output voltage of an amplifier is 1,000,000 times greater than the input, the difference in intensity level is

$$20 \log \frac{V_2}{V_1} = 20 \log 1,000,000$$

$$= 20 \log 10^6 = 20(6) = 120 \text{ dB}$$

Table 1.1. Approximate Intensity Levels for Various Sounds

120 dB	threshold of pain
110	loud thunder
100	riveting
90	noisy factory
80	
70	busy traffic
60	conversation
50	
40	quiet home
30	
20	
10	quiet whisper
0	threshold of hearing

Source: J. J. Josephs, *The Physics of Musical Sound*, p. 40; © 1967 Litton Educ. Publ., Inc. Reprinted by permission of D. Van Nostrand Co.

Table 1.2. Decibel Ratings for Power, Current, and Voltage Ratios

Power Ratios	Decibels	Voltage or Current Ratio	Decibels
1	0	1	0
2	3.0	2	6.0
3	4.8	3	9.5
4	6.0	4	12.0
5	7.0	5	14.0
6	7.8	6	15.6
7	8.5	7	16.9
8	9.0	8	18.1
9	9.5	9	19.1
10	10	10	20
100	20	100	40
1,000	30	1,000	60
10,000	40	10,000	80
100,000	50	100,000	100
1,000,000	60	1,000,000	120

Source: Harry F. Olson, *Modern Sound Reproduction*, p. 16; © 1971 Litton Educ. Publ.; Inc. Reprinted by permission of Van Nostrand Reinhold Co.

This result shows that the entire dynamic range of hearing (10^{12}) is achieved by a 10^6 range in amplifier voltage gain. For comparison and reference we include Table 1.2 showing both power and voltage ratios expressed in dB.

1.7 ABOUT UNITS

In this chapter we introduce several equations and occasionally the units of the numbers in those equations. Note that only a few fundamental units occur in physics. Those of chief importance to us are:

length: meter (m)   (1 m ≈ 3.3 ft)
time: second (s)
mass (m): kilogram (kg)   (1 kg weighs 2.2 lb)
charge: coulomb (C)   (introduced in next chapter)

All other units that we use are derived units, that is, made up of these four fundamental units. For example, force is given by $F = ma$, which has units

$$\text{force: kg} \times \frac{\text{m}}{\text{s}^2} = \frac{\text{kg} \cdot \text{m}}{\text{s}^2} = \text{N} \text{ or   newton}$$

The symbol N is given to the derived unit kg·m/s² in honor of Sir Isaac Newton. To get a feeling for the size of this unit, remember that 1 N is about the weight of an apple. The customary British or engineering unit of weight, pounds (lb), correlates with the N by

1 lb = 4.4 N   or   1 N = 0.22 lb

Therefore, a person who weighs 115 lb in customary units weighs 500 N in the metric system!

Furthermore, we can calculate from force, $F = ma$, the quantities of mass and acceleration. For example, if a force of 10 N is applied to a 2-kg mass, the resulting acceleration is

$$a = \frac{F}{m} = \frac{10 \text{ N}}{2 \text{ kg}} = 5 \frac{\text{kg} \cdot \text{m}/\text{s}^2}{\text{kg}} = 5 \frac{m}{s^2}$$

Energy also has a derived unit that is given a special name. The units work out to be

$$\text{energy} = \frac{\text{kg} \cdot \text{m}^2}{\text{s}^2} = \text{N} \cdot \text{m} = \text{J} \quad \text{or} \quad \text{joule}$$

The name is given in honor of James Prescott Joule, one of the first to recognize the equivalence of different forms of energy.

Power is the rate at which energy is expended, so the units of power are derived from

$$\text{power} = \frac{\text{energy}}{\text{time}} = \frac{\text{J}}{\text{s}} = \text{W} \quad \text{or} \quad \text{watt}$$

The unit is named after James Watt, known for his invention of the steam engine.

Finally, the spring constant k has derived units. Hooke's law ($F = -kx$) requires that the units of k be N/m, which can be checked by multiplying the units of k (or N/m) by the units of x (or m) to produce the units of force (N).

1.8 SUMMARY

(1) Sound is transmitted by pressure variations called waves. In the region of space containing a sound wave, the pressure will vary above and below the average atmospheric pressure value.

(2) Waves are described by amplitude, wavelength, and frequency. The wave relation expresses the frequency and wavelength in terms of the velocity of sound:

$$f\lambda = v \qquad\qquad\qquad (1.2)$$

(3) Longitudinal waves cause particles to vibrate back and forth in the direction that the wave travels. Transverse waves cause particles to vibrate perpendicular to the direction of travel of the wave.

(4) The phenomenon of resonance produces large oscillations of the particles in a medium when standing waves are present. Standing waves have clearly defined nodes of no particle motion and antinodes of maximum motion.

(5) The term force is used to describe how one system influences another. Newton's second law relates force, mass, and acceleration:

$$F = ma \tag{1.3}$$

Mass is the amount of material in a body, and is the property of matter that causes it to resist changes in motion. Acceleration is a measure of change of motion, that is, the rate at which velocity is changing.

(6) Hooke's law describes the force that a spring exerts when pulled away from its rest position (the equilibrium position):

$$F = -kx \tag{1.4}$$

The spring constant k is a measure of the strength of the spring and x is the displacement away from equilibrium. The minus sign indicates that a spring always exerts a force oppositely directed to the displacement of the spring.

(7) Systems that obey Hooke's law oscillate with simple harmonic motion at a frequency of

$$f = \frac{1}{2\pi}\sqrt{\frac{k}{m}} \tag{1.5}$$

(8) Intensity describes how much energy falls on a certain area in a certain amount of time. Since power is the rate at which energy is delivered (energy per unit time), intensity is also equal to power per unit area. Intensity, energy, and power in a wave all depend on the square of the frequency and the square of the amplitude of the wave.

(9) Large numbers are sometimes conveniently expressed by logarithms. The decibel notation is one such use of logarithms for expressing the ratio of intensities of two sounds. The difference in intensity level is

$$L_2 - L_1 = 10 \log \frac{I_2}{I_1} \tag{1.9}$$

where L_2 is the intensity level of the second sound, etc. Since intensity can be related to the square of voltage, a similar relation may be expressed for voltage ratios:

$$L_2 - L_1 = 20 \log \frac{V_2}{V_1} \tag{1.10}$$

QUESTIONS

1. What happens to the molecules in air when a sound wave passes? What happens to the atoms in a steel beam when a sound wave travels along the beam?

2. We mentioned that the speed of sound in air is 345 m/s when the air is at room temperature. When the air is higher in temperature, v_s is higher. When the air is colder, v_s is lower. Try to explain why this is so.

3. Why are all sound waves in air longitudinal waves?
4. What is mass? How much mass does your body have?
5. What is acceleration? How does it relate to force? Can there be an acceleration without a force?
6. What is physical work? How does energy relate to work?
7. What does energy per unit volume mean? How is the energy in a sound wave in air passed through the air? What role do the air molecules play in transferring this energy?
8. How are intensity and energy related?
9. Is an increase of 20 dB a large or small increase? What is the significance of "deci" in decibel? Why do we use the dB scale?
10. Review Hooke's law. Why is it so important in a study of sound reproduction? What does the k in the law signify?

EXERCISES

1. Calculate the wavelengths for sound in air at room temperature for the two extreme audible frequencies, 20 Hz and 17,000 Hz. (The normal upper auditory limit for humans may be anywhere between 10,000 and 20,000 Hz, depending on age, sex, etc.) (First answer: 17.2 m)
2. A sound wave in air has a wavelength of 0.5 m (about 1.5 ft). What is the frequency of the sound?
3. Using electronic equipment in a very large auditorium, a technician measures 0.10 s for the sound from a cymbals player onstage to reach the technician's listening position. What is the separation distance between the cymbals and the technician? (Answer: 34.5 m)
4. A sound wave leaves a loudspeaker, travels to the rear wall of a room, echoes back, and returns to the position of the loudspeaker in 2×10^{-2} s. What is the distance from the speaker to the rear wall?
5. A sound wave in a small room with walls 2 m apart is creating a standing wave through the resonance phenomenon. Assuming that the frequency of the sound is such that the standing wave has displacement nodes at the walls and nowhere else, calculate the frequency of the sound. (Answer: 86.2 Hz)
6. What is the next highest frequency that will produce resonance between the walls of the room in Exercise 5? (Hint: Draw a wave pattern with nodes at the walls. The longest wave you can draw is the lowest frequency, the fundamental. This wave is shorter.)
7. (a) What is the acceleration of a mass of 2 kg when acted on by a force of 4 N? (b) What is the acceleration of a mass of 2 gm when acted on by the same force? (First answer: 2 m/s²)
8. Suppose the force necessary to cause a turntable stylus to accelerate at 2 m/s² is 10^{-4} N. What is the mass of the stylus?
9. A spring has a force constant of 10 N/m. How much force is required to stretch the spring 1 cm? (Answer: 0.1 N)
10. The suspension of a certain loudspeaker has a spring constant of

25 N/m. What force must the driver of the loudspeaker supply to drive the cone 0.5 cm from its rest position?

11. Suppose a loudspeaker has a cone mass of 0.25 gm and a suspension spring constant of 6.25 N/m. What is the natural frequency of vibration of the system? (These numbers are not practical but were chosen to make the arithmetic simpler.) (Answer: 0.7 Hz)

12. A sound generator is rated to have an average power of 20 W. How much energy can this device produce in 5 s?

13. What happens to the energy per unit volume in a sound wave if you double the frequency but hold the amplitude constant?

14. The energy per unit volume in air containing a sound wave of frequency f is 10 J/m³ when the displacement of the air particles is known to be 0.005 cm. If a louder sound of the same frequency causes a displacement of 0.01 cm, how much energy per unit volume does the louder sound contain? (Answer: 40 J/m³)

15. If a certain amount of sound energy falling on an area of 10^{-4} m² each second produces an intensity of 10^{-4} W/m², what is the intensity produced by three times as much energy falling on the same area in the same time?

16. A stereo system is producing energy at a rate of 20 W. How great must the power of the system be to produce a sound "twice as loud" as the first? (An increase in intensity level of sound of 10 dB is commonly interpreted as "twice as loud.")

17. Two sounds are 20 dB different in intensity level. If the intensity of the weaker is I, what is the intensity of the louder? (Answer: 100 I)

18. Two signals in an amplifier differ by 20 dB. If the voltage of the weaker is V, what is the voltage of the stronger?

19. A certain spring system is known to vibrate at a frequency of 20 Hz. If we increase the mass on the spring to four times its original value, what will the new frequency be? (Answer: 10 Hz)

2
RECORDING TRANSDUCERS

2.1 INTRODUCTION

We have seen that a sound wave carries energy. For the purpose of storing or transmitting that energy we must have some device that will transform the acoustic energy to some other form. Any device that will perform this function is called a *transducer*.

Our conditioned response to such a need is to think of the acousto-electric transducer, the microphone. Before discussing microphones, let us note that microphones are not the only possibilities for transducers. For example, magnetic pickups on electric guitars do not transform sound in air to electrical impulses but rather the *vibration of the guitar strings themselves*. No "air sound" is involved!

Also, consider a large, thin plate supported at three corners as shown in Fig. 2.1. The fourth corner is attached to a cutting tool which in turn can cut a groove in a wax cylinder. As a sound wave strikes the plate, the high pressure region of the wave pushes the plate causing a displacement of the cutting stylus. As the sound wave progresses, the high pressure region passes behind the plate with the low pressure, rarified region in front. Thus the plate is pushed back, again displacing the cutting tool. The groove now contains stored information: a perma-

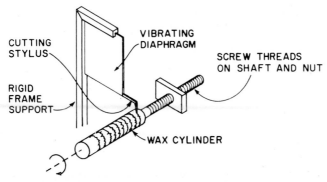

Fig. 2.1. Mechanical recorder involves no acoustoelectrical conversion; energy transformation is directly acoustomechanical.

nent record of the sound wave. And no electrical impulses were ever created! This recording method does not involve acoustoelectrical conversion but rather direct acoustomechanical conversion. Devices similar in principle to this were used for recordings around 1900.

2.2 MICROPHONES

A microphone is a transducer that converts acoustic energy into electrical energy. The input is acoustic; there is physical motion of atoms. For example, in conventional recording microphones the pressure wave in air provides the energy input. For underwater recording, the motion of water molecules supplies the energy. For studying the transmission of sound in solids, microphones are cemented directly to the ends of the material to detect the motion of the atoms of the sample itself.

The output of a microphone is an electric signal. It may be in the form of a pure alternating current or as a varying-voltage, direct current (when coupled with other devices). This electric signal is ideally a perfect translation of the acoustic signal. If the difference in pressure between compressions is large, then the voltage output should be large. No matter how complicated the wave pattern of the pressure wave, the voltage output should be a faithful reproduction. Thus, the signal may be plotted as a variation of pressure in the acoustic wave or as a variation of voltage in an electric circuit as in Fig. 2.2.

2.3 VOLTAGE AS SIGNAL

Let us digress to discuss the meaning of voltage and how it can carry a signal. In Chapter 1, we define energy as the ability to do work or the ability to move something. Such an ability involves some type of force. For an acoustic signal the force is transmitted by the physical contact of the moving air molecules colliding with, say, a diaphragm.

Electrical force results simply from the presence of electric charge. It is well known that two like charges, electrons for example, will repel each other and two unlike charges, an electron and a proton for ex-

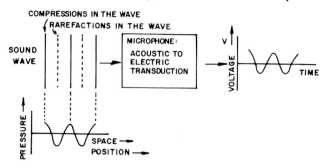

Fig. 2.2. Symbolic diagram showing conversion of sound wave (also plotted as pressure variation) to varying-voltage signal.

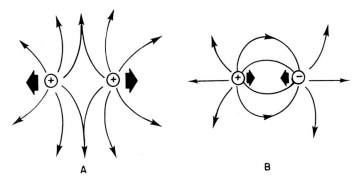

Fig. 2.3. Electric field diagrams. A: Two positive charges. B: Positive charge and negative charge. Heavy arrows show forces on charges: repulsion in A and attraction in B.

ample, will attract one another. Each charge causes a force on every other charge. Furthermore, we know that it is not necessary for the charges to be touching for this electrical force to occur. The proper way to describe this property is through the concept of an *electric field*. When a charge is present, an electric field exists in space so that another charge brought into this region will experience a force. In Fig. 2.3A we show two like charges and the electric field lines resulting from their presence. The electric field lines indicate the direction of the force a third charge would experience at any point in this same region. In Fig. 2.3B two unlike charges are shown indicating the attractive forces and electric field lines. Electric field lines emanate from positive charges and terminate on negative charges.

How does all this cause a current to flow in a circuit? A conductor is a material in which an abundance of electrons are relatively free to move (provided they stay inside the conductor). Each electron experiences the electric fields of all other electrons in the material, but since there are essentially equal distributions of electrons on each side of a single electron, the net force on that electron is zero—for every electric force trying to drive an electron in one direction along the conductor, there is an equal and opposite force trying to drive it in the opposite direction.

Now suppose by some means an excess of electrons is accumulated at one end of the conductor. Then, because the distributions are not equal, an electron in the conductor will experience a net force being repelled by the accumulated charge, and the electron will move in response to that force. So will other electrons in the conductor. The result is a flow of charge, which is a *current*.

Let us present another explanation for the flow of charge in a circuit. It is analogous to a ball rolling down a hill from a point of high energy to a point of low energy. Charges, likewise, flow from points of high to low (minimum) energy.

However, it is not convenient to discuss the energy of charges in a circuit because the amount of energy depends on the amount of charge; twice as much charge has twice as much energy. To eliminate the inconvenience of calculating energy while retaining the convenience of the energy description of charges moving from points of high to low energy, we introduce the term *voltage*. Voltage is related to the energy difference between points; in fact, if there is a voltage difference between two points we know there is an energy difference for charges moved between those points. The motivation for using voltage is that it is characteristic of the circuit, not the charge flowing in the circuit.

For example, suppose the voltage difference between two points in a circuit is $V = 10$ V; that is, the first point has 0 V and the second point has 10 V. How much energy would be required to move a single electron from one point to the other? To calculate that energy, we need to know the charge of the electron e. This physical quantity is well known: -1.6×10^{-19} C. The equation relating difference in energy between two points and the voltage between those points is

difference in energy = charge times voltage
$$E_2 - E_1 = e(V_2 - V_1) \tag{2.1}$$

For our example,

$$E_2 - E_1 = (-1.6 \times 10^{-19} \text{ C}) (10 \text{ V}) = -1.6 \times 10^{-18} \text{ J}$$

The magnitude of the result is not important for this discussion. The important point is that the result is negative. We do not have to supply energy to the electron for it to move from one point to the other! The electron moves in response to the electric field. On the other hand, to bring the electron back from the second point to the first does require energy:

$$
\begin{aligned}
E_1 - E_2 &= e(V_1 - V_2) \\
&= (-1.6 \times 10^{-19} \text{ C}) (0 - 10) \text{ V} \\
&= (-1.6 \times 10^{-19} \text{ C}) (-10 \text{ V}) = +1.6 \times 10^{-18} \text{ J}
\end{aligned}
$$

This illustration demonstrates how voltage may be used to calculate energy changes. Knowing that the process is possible, we no longer need to do the calculation. If we know the voltages in a circuit, we know how every electron in the circuit will behave.

It is appropriate here to mention the conventions used for describing voltage. A site of accumulated positive charge is said to have positive voltage with reference to a point having no charge accumulation. Furthermore, *conventional current* is the flow of positive charge from a high voltage site to a low voltage site. This is an unfortunate choice, because we know that in real circuits it is *electrons* that flow, not positive charge, and they flow from negative to positive voltage points. Thus, we have a dilemma: do we discuss conventional current flow or do we discuss electron flow? In this book we discuss electron flow, because it is the correct description of the real situation. Our diagrams indicate the direction electrons would pass; conventional current would flow in the opposite direction. For example, a battery may employ chemical forces to cause electrons to accumulate at one terminal, causing a difference in voltage from the other terminal. If a wire is connected between the two terminals, electrons will flow from the negative end (where many electrons have been accumulated) through the wire to the positive (electron-deficient) terminal.

Finally, a changing voltage between two points in a circuit can carry a signal. For positive voltage electrons move from one terminal to the other. If the polarity of the voltage signal is reversed, the direction of the electron flow reverses. If the magnitude of the voltage is large, many electrons flow. If the voltage difference between the terminals is zero, no electrons flow. Thus, a voltage signal can cause a varying electron flow in the circuit, and that varying electron flow carries all the information of the original signal.

2.4 MAGNETIC MICROPHONE

We will now consider the devices used for the transduction of acoustic energy into electrical energy—the various types of microphones. One of the most common microphones is the dynamic magnetic microphone shown in Fig 2.4.

Suppose an acoustic wave strikes this microphone. The high pressure region of the wave pushes the diaphragm inward causing the voice coil to move in the strong magnetic field between the magnet and the iron pole piece. This motion of a coil in a magnetic field creates a voltage in the coil by a process called *induction*.

To understand induction let us go back to the basic physics of charged particles, for example, electrons. We know that when two electrons are at rest, they repel each other. What happens if they are mov-

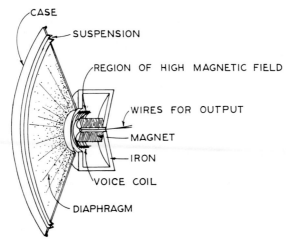

Fig. 2.4.   Cutaway drawing of dynamic magnetic microphone.

ing? Of course, they still have a repulsion, but because they are moving, new phenomena take place. Whenever a charged particle moves, it creates a magnetic field. We are not concerned at this point with the magnitude of the associated magnetism but only that it exists.

Now, because the moving electron has its own magnetic field, it can interact with other external magnetic fields, just as two compasses interact with each other. Furthermore, the result of the interaction is a force on the electron perpendicular to both the direction of motion of the electron and the direction of the magnetic field. Consider Fig. 2.5 which shows an electron moving in a magnetic field. The direction of the magnetic field is from the north pole to the south pole, and the direction of the motion of the electron is across the gap between the poles. The resulting force on the electron is up, perpendicular to the other two forces.

To see how this phenomenon is used in the dynamic magnetic microphone, remember that a conductor (the voice coil in the microphone) has free electrons in it, as discussed previously. From Fig 2.6 we see that if we move a vertical wire through the space between the pole pieces of the magnet, each electron in the wire will experience a force driving the electron along the wire. Thus, while the wire is moving in the magnetic field, electrons are forced to the top of the wire. The result is an accumulation of electrons at the top and a deficiency at the bottom, which is in effect a voltage difference along the wire. If we connect an external circuit to the top and bottom of the wire, electron current would flow in that circuit. If the wire stops moving, the force is removed and the electrons stop flowing in the external circuit. If the wire is moved in the opposite direction to that shown in Fig. 2.6, the force will be downward and the electrons will reverse their direction of flow.

In the dynamic magnetic microphone the motion of the diaphragm causes the voice coil to move in and out of the magnetic field of the magnet. Thus electrons are caused to flow in the voice coil each time the coil moves. Connecting an external circuit to the output leads will allow an external flow of electrons having the same signal characteristics as the original acoustic wave.

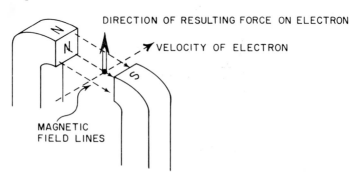

Fig. 2.5.   Net force (up) on free electron passing across magnetic field.

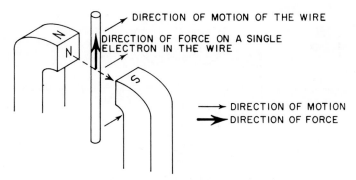

Fig. 2.6. Net force on electron in wire when wire is passed across magnetic field.

In principle we could design another type of magnetic microphone, a *moving magnet* microphone. In Fig. 2.7 we show a suggested sketch of the instrument. The magnet is rigidly fixed to the diaphragm so that all diaphragm motion is repeated by the magnet. Thus, the changing magnetic field cuts across the fixed voice coil. The physical description is no different from the dynamic magnetic microphone however, since electrons cutting across the field lines or field lines cutting across electrons are just two ways of looking at the same phenomenon.

A third type of magnetic microphone has both the magnet and the coil fixed. In Fig. 2.8 we see that there is a piece of magnetic material attached to the diaphragm that transmits the magnetic field from the permanent magnet to the voice coil. As the diaphragm moves this piece also moves and changes the distribution of the magnetic field in the region of the voice coil, thus inducing an electron flow as in the above cases.

2.5 CRYSTAL OR CERAMIC MICROPHONE

The crystal microphone employs the phenomenon of *piezoelectricity* as a voltage-generating mechanism. In crystal form, materials such as barium titanate, lead sulphate, and Rochelle salt exhibit the property of a voltage difference spontaneously appearing between the two faces of the crystal if the crystal is bent. Such materials are called piezoelec-

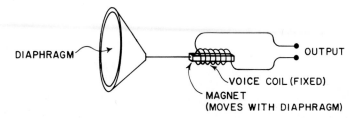

Fig. 2.7. Sketch of primary parts of moving magnet (dynamic) microphone.

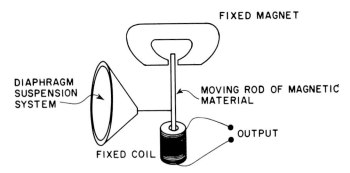

Fig. 2.8.   Sketch of microphone with both magnet and coil fixed.

trics and provide a simple means of acoustoelectric transduction. (See Fig. 2.9.)

The crystal is mounted with three corners rigidly supported. The diaphragm is connected to the crystal at the free corner. Also, small plates to which wires are connected to carry the output voltage signal may be attached to the crystal. As the sound wave moves the diaphragm, the crystal distorts and a voltage is generated across the output leads. In the ideal case, the voltage is directly proportional to the size of the distortion; that is, for large amplitude sound waves a large amplitude voltage signal is generated.

2.6   CARBON MICROPHONE

Perhaps the most common of all microphones is the carbon microphone employed in telephone handsets. This microphone is different from the above types in that it does not generate voltage but rather changes current flow through it.

Section 2.3 concerns how voltage differences cause current flow. A useful relation describing the current flow through a given piece of material is Ohm's law:

$$V = IR \tag{2.2}$$

where V is the voltage difference across the body, I is the current flowing through the body, and R is the resistance of the body. This law is very

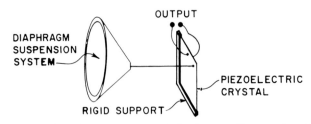

Fig. 2.9.   Crystal microphone. Motion of diaphragm distorts piezoelectric crystal, generating voltage between crystal faces.

important. In effect, it says that if we put a given voltage across a body, the rate of flow of electrons in the body (current) will be governed by a particular property of the body (resistance). If a body has high resistance, it will be difficult for electrons to flow through it, and the number of electrons passing through in a given amount of time is relatively small. On the other hand a material with low resistance will allow high currents to pass through it.

Most of us are aware that V is measured in volts and the current I is measured in amperes (A). The unit of resistance is the ohm and is symbolized by Ω. We can use Ohm's law to calculate V, I, or R, given the other two. For example, if a 10-V battery is connected to a 20-Ω resistor, a current of 0.5 A will flow, because

$$V = IR$$

$$I = \frac{V}{R} = \frac{10 \text{ V}}{20 \text{ }\Omega} = 0.5 \text{ A}$$

If the resistance were reduced to 10 Ω, a current of 1 A would flow. The smaller the resistance is, the larger the current is.

The current I is the same whether we speak of conventional current or electron flow—there is no ambiguity. For example, 1 A equals 1 C of charge passing a point in 1 s. If we say $I = 2A$, we mean either 2 C of positive charge are passing some point each second in one direction or 2 C of electrons are passing some point each second in the opposite direction. Both are described by I.

The carbon microphone has a chamber filled with carbon granules. If the granules are tightly packed, the resistance of the chamber to a flow of electrons is small. If the granules are loosely packed the resistance is high. Thus the carbon microphone has a variable resistance, depending on the density of the carbon granules. If one wall of the chamber holding the granules is connected to a diaphragm, the sound waves moving the diaphragm will in turn change the density of the carbon and vary the resistance. If a voltage difference is supplied across the granules, the current flow will vary as the audio signal.

It is not necessary to discuss carbon microphones as varying-current output devices. We can treat them as varying-output voltage devices, as indicated in Fig. 2.10. To understand this, consider the following. Suppose we have a voltage source, a battery for example, connected to two resistances connected in series as in Fig. 2.11. (Note that the circuit symbol for resistance is a jagged line indicating the difficulty the electrons have in passing through the resistor.)

Each electron flowing out of the battery must pass through both resistors. Thus the current through R_1 must equal the current through R_2, which must equal the total current flow through the circuit. We have, then,

$$I_{\text{total}} = I_1 = I_2$$

or, from Eq. (2.2),

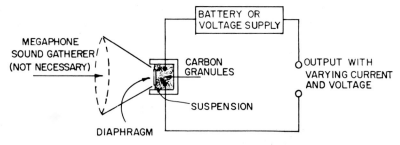

Fig. 2.10. Carbon microphone.

$$\frac{V_{\text{battery}}}{R_{\text{total}}} = \frac{V_1}{R_1} = \frac{V_2}{R_2}$$

Here, V_1 represents the voltage drop across resistance R_1. It is a drop because the electrons lose energy when passing through a resistance.

The total voltage gain by the electrons in the battery must be equal to the total voltage loss of the electrons in the resistances. (If they gained more than they lost, they would become more and more energetic on each pass through the circuit; if they lost more than they gained, they could never make it back to the battery.) Therefore,

$$V_{\text{battery}} = V_1 + V_2 \quad \text{or} \quad IR_{\text{total}} = IR_1 + IR_2$$

which can only be true if

$$R_{\text{total}} = R_1 + R_2 \tag{2.3}$$

Equation (2.3) is true for a series circuit, in which the total resistance is the sum of individual resistances.

In a practical circuit containing a carbon microphone, the resistor R_1 might represent the microphone and R_2 might represent the load, such as an amplifier or headphone, etc. The resistance R_2 does not change; the resistance R_1 of course does change as the sound wave compresses the carbon granules in the microphone. Therefore, the total resistance, $R = R_1 + R_2$, changes. The result is that the total current I flowing in the circuit is variable, since

$$I = \frac{V}{R} = \frac{\text{voltage of battery, constant}}{\text{total resistance, varying}}$$

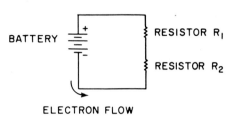

ELECTRON FLOW

Fig. 2.11. Series resistance circuit.

If the current varies, the voltage drop across the load resistor R_2 will vary, since

$$V_{\text{load}} = IR_2$$

If the load were a voltmeter, we would see the needle indicating varying voltage. Or the load might be the input circuit of an amplifier, and we might drive a loudspeaker with the amplified alternating signal. Thus, the variable resistance carbon microphone can be used to produce a varying voltage.

2.7   CONDENSER OR ELECTROSTATIC MICROPHONE

Another type of microphone that does not generate voltage is the condenser or electrostatic microphone, which uses the property of a condenser (or capacitor) to vary the input voltage.

Suppose we have a constant voltage supply such as a battery. We connect wires to the battery and to two conducting plates as shown in Fig. 2.12. The plates are separated from each other and originally have no charge on them. The negative terminal of the battery is a source of excess accumulated electrons, so some electrons flow along the wire to the right-hand plate, making it negative. The positive terminal of the battery is deficient in electrons, and some of the free electrons on the attached plate flow to the battery, leaving the plate positive. The final result is a static charge, which is negative on one plate, positive on the other.

The amount of charge stored by this capacitor is again a property of the body. If the plates are large, they hold more charge. If the plates are close together, the attraction between the positive and negative charges will allow more charge to flow from the battery and collect. The amount of final charge on each plate is given by

$$Q = CV \tag{2.4}$$

where Q is the charge, C is the *capacitance* and V is the voltage of the battery.

Now let us remove the battery and put a voltage-measuring device such as a voltmeter across the terminals (see Fig. 2.13). The voltmeter reads voltage V given by

$$V = Q_{\text{stored}}/C$$

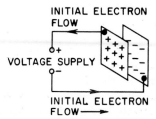

Fig. 2.12.   Two parallel capacitor plates being charged by battery. Plates are separated and therefore insulated from each other.

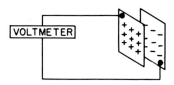

Fig. 2.13.   Measuring voltage across charged capacitor.

Recall that Q_{stored} is constant. Note that because the capacitance C is a property of the body, we can change C and therefore change V. For example, let us move the plates closer together. The capacitance C becomes larger and V becomes smaller. If we pull the plates apart, C becomes smaller and V becomes larger.

We can now construct a capacitor microphone by rigidly mounting one plate, attaching the second plate to a diaphragm, and storing a charge on the plates. As the diaphragm moves, the capacitance will change, and the voltage across the microphone will vary with the audio signal.

For a numerical example, suppose we have a capacitor of 100 μF capacitance. (The unit of capacitance is the farad, which equals 1 C/V. Because the coulomb is such a large quantity of charge, the farad is also very large—too large, in fact, for useful electronics applications. The more common unit is the microfarad, equal to 10^{-6} F and written as μF.) We connect our 100-μF capacitor to a 10-V battery. How much charge will accumulate on the plates of the capacitor? By using Eq. (2.4) we find

$$Q = CV = (100 \times 10^{-6} \text{ F})(10 \text{ V}) = 10^{-3} \text{ C}$$

Now we disconnect the capacitor leaving it charged. If no other changes were made, there is a 10-V potential difference between the two plates. Suppose we now push the plates closer together so that the capacitance increases to 200 μF. What would be the new voltage between the plates?

$$V = \frac{Q}{C} = \frac{10^{-3} \text{ C}}{200 \times 10^{-6} \text{ F}} = 5 \text{ V}$$

As the capacitance is increased, the voltage is decreased.

2.8   VELOCITY (RIBBON) MICROPHONE

Although we have not explicitly stated it, each of the previous microphones responds directly to the pressure in a sound wave. The ribbon microphone, shown in Fig. 2.14, depends on the pressure in the sound wave but in a manner that also depends on the velocity of sound. To understand this, note in the drawing that both the front and the back of the ribbon (diaphragm) element are exposed. Part of the sound wave follows path (1) directly to the ribbon. Another part of the sound wave follows path (2), bending around the microphone case and magnet and approaching the ribbon from the rear. Because path (2) is

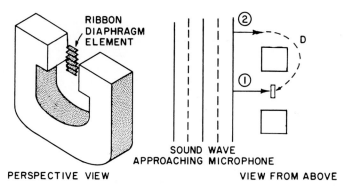

RIBBON
DIAPHRAGM
ELEMENT

SOUND WAVE
APPROACHING MICROPHONE

PERSPECTIVE VIEW   VIEW FROM ABOVE

Fig. 2.14. Two schematic views of ribbon microphone. On right, sound wave is shown approaching microphone; D is increased length wave must travel along path (2) to reach ribbon.

longer, the wave front reaches the rear of the ribbon later than the part of the wave front following path (1) reaches the front of the ribbon. As a result, the sound waves in front of and behind the ribbon are always out of phase, causing a pressure difference between the front and back of the ribbon. This pressure difference causes a displacement of the conducting ribbon in the magnetic field, which in turn causes a voltage to be generated across the ribbon.

The name of velocity microphone stems from the fact that the phase difference between the front and back of the ribbon depends on the velocity of sound. The phase difference can be calculated from the simple relation that distance traveled equals velocity times time. The time delay between the front and back parts of the wave, then, is

$$t = D/v$$

where D is the distance along path (2) and v is the velocity of sound. Clearly, the time delay depends on the velocity of sound.

Another interesting consideration for this microphone arises because the front and back are both open. Suppose a sound wave approaches the microphone from the side as shown in Fig. 2.15. Note that the wave striking the ribbon from the right exactly cancels the pressure on the ribbon from the wave striking from the left. The result is that, even though a sound wave is present, no pressure difference exists between the two sides of the ribbon, and the ribbon does not move. This type of microphone construction eliminates response to waves approaching from the side. Such types of construction can be used to develop directional response characteristics in microphones.

2.9 MICROPHONE DIRECTIONAL CHARACTERISTICS

We have shown in Fig. 2.15 that a wave approaching the microphone from the right side of the drawing would have the same response as a wave from the left. Thus, the ribbon microphone is said to have a

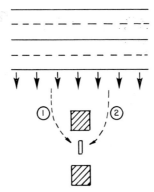

Fig. 2.15. Sound wave approaching open-backed ribbon microphone from side.

bidirectional response. This bidirectional response characteristic of the ribbon microphone is shown in Fig. 2.16A. The solid lines indicate that all equally loud sources at positions on those lines would produce the same loudness response. The cardioid pattern of B is useful for recording live performances of, say, a choir. If the microphone is aimed towards the performers, extraneous noises such as coughs from the audience will be minimized. The highly directional pattern in C is appropriate for specialized recording needs, such as for sensing sounds from a distant source when the source is weak relative to the background noise. Occasionally such systems are seen on televised football games where the technician on the sidelines is attempting to record the calls from the quarterback on the field.

Another interesting use of cardioid or directional microphones is to eliminate squeal in a public address system. We have all heard instances where a PA system would begin to scream; usually the person speaking is desperate to correct the problem. The scream arises when

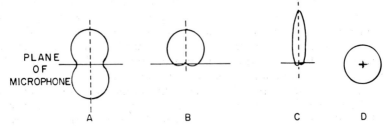

Fig. 2.16. Directivity characteristics of various microphones. Patterns represent positions around microphones that cause same strength of response. A: Bidirectional cardioid pattern for ribbon microphones. B: Normal unidirectional cardioid pattern. C: Highly directive unidirectional cardioid pattern. D: Omnidirectional pattern.

the microphone picks up sound from the loudspeaker, the sound is reamplified, picked up again, and so on. As the process continues, the sound gets louder and louder, finally to reach the scream level. This phenomenon is usually caused by position of the microphone in front or to the side of a loudspeaker. Thus, two solutions are available— move the microphone or loudspeaker (sometimes not possible because of permanent mountings) or use cardioid (directional) microphones aimed to have minimal response in the direction of the loudspeaker.

Finally, Fig. 2.16D indicates a response pattern for an omnidirectional microphone, appropriate for recording a round table discussion with the microphone in the center of the table. Note that the cardioid pattern microphones (B) can be used for this purpose if placed pointing upward on the table. The axis of the cardioid pattern would be vertical, and all persons sitting around the table would be equidistant from the axis and the microphone and thereby evoke equal response.

2.10 DISTORTION IN RECORDING

The technology of microphone design is sufficiently advanced to obtain very high quality acoustoelectrical transduction. In fact, the microphone may not be the chief limiting or distortive device in an audio system. However, we should examine areas of potential distortion possible in microphones.

Imagine the difficult task of recording a large orchestra. The dynamic range of intensity produced by such a group may vary as much as 60 dB, meaning that the intensity ratio of the sound produced by every instrument playing at full volume as compared to the faint sounds of a single woodwind soloist may be as great as 10^6. Thus, the microphone is called on to reproduce faithfully a range of 1 to 10^6 in intensity. Recall that power and intensity depend on the square of voltage, so that the 10^6 range in intensity means a corresponding microphone output voltage range of 1000. Let us examine one particular type of microphone to gain appreciation for this wide voltage range.

We have considered the structure of the dynamic magnetic microphone (Fig. 2.4), but we have not investigated the relation between the amplitude of the displacement of the diaphragm to the voltage output. The voltage output of a dynamic magnetic microphone is given by

$$V = Blv \tag{2.5}$$

where: V = output voltage
  B = magnetic field intensity of magnet in microphone
  l = length of microphone voice coil
  v = velocity of voice coil as it oscillates in magnetic field of microphone magnet

Before we can use Eq. (2.5), we must know the velocity v. Velocity is given (see Olson: *Modern Sound Reproduction*) by

$$v = \frac{pA}{Z_m} \tag{2.6}$$

where: p = sound pressure incident on microphone
$\quad\quad\ A$ = area of diaphragm
$\quad\quad\ Z_m$ = mechanical impedance (or resistance) of diaphragm-sus-
$\quad\quad\quad\ $ pension system. (Impedance is discussed at length in Chap
$\quad\quad\quad\ $ ter 4.)

Thus, if the sound pressure p changes, the velocity v changes. And if v changes, the output voltage V changes.

If we examine Eqs. (2.5) and (2.6) we can understand some of the reasons why a microphone will have difficulty in reproducing a dynamic range of 10^6. Two reasons are as follows:

(1) The mechanical impedance Z_m is a type of mechanical resistance; that is, Z_m is related to the stiffness with which the diaphragm is suspended from the microphone case. If the pressure in the sound wave varies by a factor of 1000, then the amplitude of the displacement of the diaphragm will also vary by a factor of 1000. For the very large displacements resulting from loud sounds, the diaphragm will be moved so far away from its equilibrium position that considerable strain will be placed on the suspension system that binds the diaphragm to the microphone case—perhaps so much strain that the value of Z_m will change. There will be some upper limit to the displacement beyond which Z_m will vary. Once Z_m changes, Eq. (2.6) says that the velocity of the diaphragm will no longer be linearly related to the pressure. A doubling of the pressure p will *not* result in a doubling of the velocity v, since Z_m also changes as pressure increases. A type of distortion has resulted.

(2) In Eq. (2.5) the l represented the length of the voice coil. However, only the portion of the voice coil actually in the region of high magnetic field intensity B has significant magnetic induction, such that the l in the equation actually describes that length. Recall that the displacement of the diaphragm may be very large for loud sounds, so that the voice coil moves out of the region of high magnetic field intensity. The result will be a shortening of the effective length l and a changing value of B as the coil moves away from the region of uniform magnetic field between the pole pieces of the magnet. Again, we have created a final voltage output of the microphone that does not linearly change with the pressure of the sound wave for very loud sounds.

Another possibility for distortion is in the frequency response of a microphone. The ideal microphone has an equal response for all frequencies; that is, if two sounds of different frequencies but the same sound pressure are incident on a microphone, the voltage output would

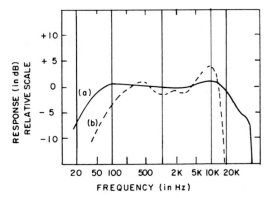

Fig. 2.17. Response in dB of two microphones to constant-pressure input sounds of varying frequency. Curve (a) shows acceptable response across most of audio spectrum; note "roll-off" in low frequency region. Curve (b) shows unacceptable response due to resonant peak at 10,000 Hz. This microphone could be advertised as "±4 dB 100–13,000 Hz."

be the same for both sounds (see Fig. 2.17). Note from Eq. (2.6) that this requires the mechanical impedance Z_m to be independent of frequency or the mechanical system of diaphragm and suspension to vibrate as freely at say 10,000 Hz as at 100 Hz. By using such tricks as combinations of several materials, adding resistance to the flow of air behind the diaphragm, etc., it is possible to produce a uniform mechanical impedance over a particular frequency range. In addition, the mechanical system and the air in the enclosed microphone case may combine to produce a resonant frequency at which the displacement of the diaphragm becomes quite large, even for soft sounds (see Fig. 2.18). Such behavior may be controlled by installing proper damping devices in the microphone.

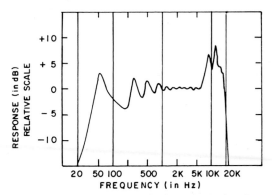

Fig. 2.18. Response of undamped ribbon microphone showing many resonant peaks. Proper mechanical damping could produce flat response from about 40 Hz to 17,000 Hz. (From M. L. Gayford, 1970, *Electroacoustics*, Newnes-Butterworths, London, p. 154. Used by permission.)

A particular microphone may have only a limited range of the frequency spectrum over which it gives "flat" response. Consider the carbon microphone of Section 2.6. At very high frequencies the packing of the carbon granules cannot mechanically follow the mechanical motion of the diaphragm. Thus at high frequencies the packing of the granules becomes essentially constant, even though the diaphragm is vibrating. The result is that the resistance of the carbon hardly changes and causes very little voltage variation at the output terminals. This limited frequency range for the carbon microphone does not restrict its being a useful device, especially in speech communication where the essential frequencies are usually within the range of the microphone.

2.11 GUITAR PICKUP

This chapter begins with a brief discussion of devices other than microphones that can be used in recording. The electric guitar pickup is one of the most common examples of these devices. Having discussed the effect of changing magnetic fields on electrons in conducting wires in Section 2.4, we understand enough of the basic physics to discuss guitar pickups.

Figure 2.19 is a sketch of a guitar pickup under a guitar string. For the system to serve as a pickup, the string must be made of a magnetizable material—a material "permeable" to a magnetic field. The operation of the pickup is as follows: the center rod is a permanent magnet that creates a magnetic field in all space, particularly in the region of the coil and the guitar string. The guitar string becomes magnetized in response to the field. When the string is set into vibration as the instrument is played, the magnetized string will oscillate and thereby disturb the distribution of the magnetic field. In particular, the field will vary in the vicinity of the coil, and we know that a varying field will induce a varying voltage and electron flow in the coil.

The guitar pickup is sensitive to the variation of the magnetic field, not to the pressure of a sound wave. Consequently, electric guitars often do not have an acoustic resonant chamber but are simply strings stretched on a supporting frame.

2.12 SUMMARY

(1) Transducers are devices that convert one form of energy to another. Microphones are transducers that convert acoustic signals into electrical signals.

(2) Charged particles exert force on each other via an electric field. Like charges repel one another; opposite charges attract. Voltage can be used as a convenient method of describing the energy a charge has in the presence of an electric field. A varying voltage can carry as an electrical signal all the information of an acoustical signal.

(3) Moving charges possess magnetic fields as well as electric fields. Thus a moving charge will interact with a magnetic field. Also, a changing magnetic field will exert a force on a stationary charge. Magnetic

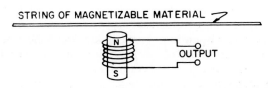

Fig. 2.19. Pickup for electric guitar. Motion of magnetizable wire causes magnetic field to change in the coil; changing field induces alternating flow of electrons in coil.

microphones depend either on the motion of a wire in the presence of a magnetic field or on the variation of a field in the presence of a coil to induce a changing voltage in the coil.

(4) Piezoelectric materials spontaneously create a front-to-back voltage difference when bent or distorted.

(5) Ohm's law relates the amount of current I flowing through a body to the voltage V and the resistance R of the body:

$$V = IR \qquad (2.2)$$

Carbon microphones have variable resistance (due to loose packing of carbon particles) in response to the varying pressure in a sound wave. Thus for a constant input voltage V, the output current varies as does the sound wave pressure p.

(6) A capacitor stores charge on two insulated plates. The amount of charge that may be stored depends on the input voltage and the capacitance of the plates:

$$Q = CV \qquad (2.4)$$

For a fixed amount of charge Q, moving the plates closer to or farther from each other will vary the capacitance and therefore the voltage between the plates. The condenser or electrostatic microphones use this technique to produce a varying-voltage signal.

(7) Ribbon microphones employ the phase difference of a single sound wave admitted into the microphone along two different paths to create directional microphone response patterns.

(8) Distortion in microphone response can occur for many reasons, such as variation of suspension stiffness with frequency or amplitude, variation of effective coil length in magnetic microphones (due to large amplitude motion), or resonance in the mechanical parts of the microphone.

(9) Electric guitar pickups depend on the motion of a magnetized guitar string to produce a changing magnetic field in a coil, thereby inducing a varying voltage in the coil.

QUESTIONS

1. What is a transducer?
2. We have discussed the principles behind the acoustoelectric trans-

ducers known as microphones. List other types of transducers commonly found in a stereo system.

3. If a microphone suspension system is known to be linear, what can be said about the shape of the electrical output waveform as compared to the acoustical input waveform?

4. Given the following conditions for a particular point in space, what can you say about the motion of an electron released at that point in space?
    (a) an electric field exists there
    (b) the electric field is pointing north

5. You wish to record a guitarist on stage in live performance. You need maximum frequency response and as much extraneous noise rejection as possible. Describe microphone types and response patterns that would be appropriate.

6. Describe how you would record a live performance of a stage play. Particular problems of such production include audience noise rejection and uniform microphone response over the whole stage.

7. Pretend you are a salesperson (an honest one). You are asked to sell the microphone whose response curve is shown as the dashed line in Fig. 2.17. Name three advantages you could honestly advertise in that microphone.

8. You are the competitor of the person in Question 7. Name three disadvantages you can honestly cite in the microphone whose response curve is shown by the dashed line in Fig. 2.17.

EXERCISES

1. Suppose three charges are equally spaced in a straight line. The outer two have charge $+Q$ and the center one has charge $-Q$. Sketch the electric field lines for this arrangement and indicate the total force on each charge.

2. In Fig. 2.5 we see that an electron moving across a magnetic field experiences a force. Suppose that an electron were moving *along* a magnetic field. What would the force on the electron be? (Answer: No force)

3. In Fig. 2.6 we see that a wire moving across a magnetic field experiences an accumulation of electrons at one end. Suppose a wire were moved along a magnetic field. What would happen in the wire? Why?

4. A battery of 12 V is connected to a 40-Ω resistor. How much current flows? (Answer: 0.3 A)

5. Two resistors and a battery are connected in series as shown in Fig. 2.11. If the resistors have the values $R_1 = 50$ Ω and $R_2 = 50$ Ω and the battery is 12 V, how much current flows?

6. Two resistors and a battery are connected as in Fig. 2.11. Resistor $R_1 = 100$ Ω and the battery is 15 V. It is found that 0.1 A flows. What is the value of resistor R_2?

7. A capacitor develops a full charge of 10^{-4} C when connected to a 10-V battery. What is the capacitance of the capacitor? (Answer: 10^{-5} F or 10 μF)
8. A 10-μF capacitor is fully charged by a 10-V battery and disconnected from the battery. We then alter the capacitance of the capacitor, doubling its value to 20 μF. What would be the voltage reading across the plates of the capacitor?

3

AMPLIFICATION

3.1 ELECTRICAL POWER

We have seen that it is possible to convert acoustic energy into electrical energy in the form of a voltage output from a microphone. We have not considered the fact that the maximum voltage produced by some types of microphones may be of the order of a few millivolts (10^{-3} V). Such a small voltage is far too weak to drive a loudspeaker. Furthermore, if we remember that the maximum output will come under conditions of loudest input sound, we realize that the softest useful input sounds may be 60 dB lower in intensity. For those sounds microphone output may be a few microvolts (10^{-6} V). To make these small signal voltages useful for such purposes as driving a loudspeaker or a disc-cutting device, it is necessary to amplify the voltage, typically into the range 1–70 V.

To increase the voltage is not enough; it is power that we must finally amplify. Recall that power is defined as the energy produced by a source per unit time. Higher power means more energy in a certain amount of time. In fact, that is exactly the purpose of using public address systems: to increase the amount of energy produced by the person speaking at the time of speaking. Thus it is power, energy per unit time, that the public address system amplifies.

The expression for power in an electrical system is

$$P = IV \tag{3.1}$$

where P = power in watts, I = current in amperes, and V = voltage in volts. This equation makes it apparent that if we operate only on the voltage of a signal without concern for the current, the power in the signal may or may not be changed. For example, a simple alternating current signal applied to a transformer whose output is connected to a light bulb may "step up" the voltage in the signal but will not change the power.

Consider Fig. 3.1. The primary, or input, side of the transformer is wound around a soft-iron core. The secondary or output side is wound around the same core. Thus when electrons flow in the primary winding, they produce a magnetic field (see Section 2.4) in the coil which in turn magnetizes the soft-iron core. The core then transfers the mag-

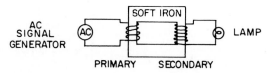

Fig. 3.1. Transformer.

netic field to the secondary coil where a current is induced. Suppose the secondary winding has five times as many turns of wire as the primary. Then the voltage induced in the secondary will be five times greater than that in the primary since the same magnetic field would cut five times as many turns of wire. But what about the current? It has dropped in the secondary, because the transformer is a device that can change voltage and current but not power. The transformer cannot add new energy to the signal. The relation between power induced by the primary (P_p) and power induced by the secondary (P_s) is

$$P_p = P_s \qquad I_p V_p = I_s V_s$$

and if $V_s = 5 V_p$, then

$$I_s = \frac{V_p}{V_s} I_p = \frac{V_p}{5V_p} I_p = \frac{I_p}{5} = 0.2I_p$$

The voltage has increased by a factor of five, but the current drops by the same factor because the power cannot change.

3.2 VACUUM TUBE AMPLIFIERS

How can we amplify power? There is no method that merely amplifies power. We can see why by the analogous situation of water flowing in a garden hose: there is no way to get more water out of the hose than is put in. However, we can use the low power signal to control a higher power signal, so that the information contained in the low power signal is superimposed on the high power system. Electronically, this is simple to do, and we shall examine such a system soon. First, we must understand the high power system that we wish to control. A diode vacuum tube is the simplest such device and is shown in Fig. 3.2. A discussion of the operation of the tube follows.

The diode vacuum tube contains two elements: a *plate* (or anode) connected to the positive side of a large voltage source and a *filament* (or cathode) connected to the negative side of the battery. In addition, the filament is heated by a current supplied by a second battery or voltage supply.

As the filament gets hot, electrons in the metal of the filament receive enough energy to escape from the metal. (They boil off like water molecules in evaporation.) This process is called *thermionic emission*. A cloud of electrons then surrounds the filament. Because the plate is positively charged and the filament is negatively charged, an electric field exists between the two elements. The cloud of electrons

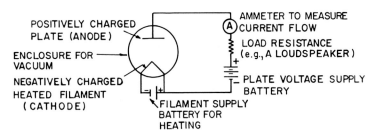

Fig. 3.2.   Diode vacuum tube in simple circuit.

responds to that field and is attracted to the plate. Thus, a current flows
through the vacuum from the cathode to the anode. The current continues to flow because the battery resupplies electrons to the cathode,
and the heat in the cathode continues to cause electrons to be emitted.

This type of tube containing two elements is called a *diode*. Note
that it will not work in reverse; that is, if the high voltage battery is reversed making the plate negative and the filament positive, no current
will flow because the plate is not hot and does not emit electrons. This
one-way property is used for *rectifier circuits* where an alternating (plus
and minus) signal is input to the diode, and only the positive portion is
conducted (see Fig. 3.3).

We are ready now to construct a hypothetical amplifier by controlling the current inside the vacuum tube. In the diode, the electrons
have an unobstructed path from the negative cathode to the positive
anode. The electrons simply follow the strong electric field lines between the elements. We now insert a third element, a wire *grid,* between
the filament and plate. We have designed the *triode* (three elements)
vacuum tube shown in Fig. 3.4. If we do not apply any voltage to the
new grid, it will have very little effect on the current flow through the
tube. The electrons will simply pass undisturbed through the openings
in the grid. However, if we apply a negative voltage to the grid, the electron flow will be diminished because the electrons being emitted by the
filament will be repelled by the negative charges on the grid. A small
negative grid voltage will diminish the current by a small amount, and
a large negative grid voltage may stop the flow altogether. In normal
operation a constant negative voltage is applied to the grid of a triode

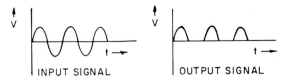

Fig. 3.3.   Input and output signals to diode tube used as rectifier; only positive
portions of input signal are passed by diode.

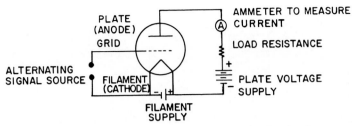

Fig. 3.4. Triode vacuum tube used as amplifier in simple circuit.

along with the small alternating signal. The result is an input signal that is always negative but varies in magnitude, preventing any appreciable current from flowing from the cathode to the grid itself.

Many types of tubes are more complicated than the simple triode. However, the basic principles we have discussed apply: a small input signal is used to control a larger signal. The British call the vacuum tube a "valve," since with it the flow of electrons can be controlled.

In summary, we have created a power amplifier: a black box that puts out a higher power signal than it receives. The amplifier may contain a single triode or perhaps several with the output (plate circuit) of each being used as input to the grid of the next tube. Thus, several stages of amplification may be employed, all housed in the black box we designate as the power amplifier.

3.3 TRANSISTOR AMPLIFIERS

Most electronic instruments produced at the present time employ solid state devices instead of vacuum tubes as the amplifying and control elements. Several advantages of these devices are immediately apparent: transistors are physically rugged whereas vacuum tubes are fragile; transistors need no heat but tubes depend on thermionic emission and must be "warmed up"; transistors are compact whereas tubes are bulky; etc. However, before we can understand how a transistor can amplify power we must examine the physics of semiconductor materials, from which transistors and other semiconducting devices are made.

3.3.1 Physics of Semiconductors

Semiconducting materials differ from conductors in fundamental ways. Consider Fig. 3.5. The upward direction in the drawing represents increasing values of energy; the horizontal direction has no significance. The drawing illustrates the *allowed energy states* (shaded regions) for electrons in three classes of solid materials. By "allowed energy states," we mean that, because of the types of atoms in the material, the symmetry with which those atoms are arranged, and the way they are bound to each other, the electrons can have only certain energies. In a metal a broad spectrum of energies is possible; in a semiconductor there is a gap in the energy spectrum (unshaded region in the drawing)

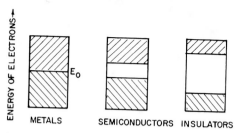

Fig. 3.5. Illustration of allowed energy states for electrons in metals, semiconductors, and insulators.

where no energy states are allowed. In an insulator, the gap is very wide.

To understand the significance of the drawing, suppose a solid is very cold—near the absolute zero of temperature. Every particle in the solid will be in a minimum energy state, because the meaning of cold is that all excess energy has been removed. Does that mean that all the particles are at zero energy? No, because of a law of physics called the _Pauli exclusion principle_. [This law requires that no two electrons can simultaneously exist in the same quantum state.] Energy is one characteristic of a quantum state; so not all electrons can be at any one energy, even zero energy. Thus, even at absolute zero many energy states are occupied, meaning electrons exist that have those energies. The line marked E_0 on the metals in Fig. 3.5 indicates the energy level to which all states are occupied at absolute zero temperature. All states below E_0 are "filled" and all states above E_0 are "unfilled." The level E_0 is called the Fermi level.

Consider the semiconductors in Fig. 3.5. At absolute zero, all the states in the lower band and none of the states in the upper band are occupied. Suppose we wish to cause a flow of electrons through the semiconductor material at absolute zero. We put an electric field across the material by means of a battery and wires attached to each end of the material. For an electron to respond to that electric field, the electron would have to change energy state, that is, increase in energy. However, it cannot change energy in a random way; it must change to another allowed energy state. In the lower band all states are occupied so that no other available state is in that band; all states are filled in the lower band. Thus, for the electron to change energy to an available (unfilled) state, the electron must have enough energy to cross the gap shown in Fig. 3.5 to an allowed energy state in the upper band. Once across the gap the electron may change energy easily and freely, since many unfilled states are available; but unless the electric field is strong enough to excite the electron across the energy gap, no conduction can take place. Thus at very cold temperatures a semiconductor does not allow conduction and is in effect an insulator.

Let us consider the same semiconductor material at room temperature. Compared to absolute zero, room temperature is quite hot, so that some electrons in the semiconductor have enough thermal energy to be in the upper, unfilled energy band. The thermal energy is sufficient to excite some electrons across the energy gap. These electrons in the upper band can contribute to conduction. If we again apply an electric field across the semiconductor, an electron flow will result because the electrons in the upper band always have allowed states available to which they may be excited. Note that the electron flow will not be as great as for a metal, since the number of electrons that have been excited across the gap to the conduction band will not be as great as the number of electrons near unfilled states in a metal where there is no energy gap at all.

We must not neglect the effects of temperature on the lower energy band. Recall that at absolute zero every allowed state in the lower band is occupied. At room temperature thermal energy has excited some electrons out of the lower band into the upper band. The effect on the lower band is that vacancies are created. These empty states in the otherwise filled lower band are commonly referred to as "holes." Consider the effect of the application of an electric field across this semiconductor material. Empty energy states or holes are in the lower band so that a few electrons in the lower band can respond to the field; that is, some electrons may change energy states into hole states. Suppose one electron changes state to fill the hole state. That means that the original state of the electron is now empty; the hole has moved. Some other electron may now fill that state so that the hole may move again. The result is that the application of an electric field to a semiconductor material at room temperature not only causes electron current flow for electrons in the upper energy band, but it also causes an effective "hole current" flow for electrons filling vacancies in the lower energy band! The holes appear to have positive charges (the absence of a negative electron), and therefore hole current flows in a direction opposite to electron current flow.

Pure semiconducting materials (such as germanium, silicon, etc.) have an equal number of conduction electrons and holes, since every hole is created by the excitation of an electron into the upper (conduction) band. It is possible to create materials that have an excess of conduction electrons or an excess of holes. Consider Fig. 3.6.

A schematic diagram representing the crystal lattice of a germanium crystal is shown in Fig. 3.6A. Note that each germanium atom is bound to four neighbors by sharing pairs of electrons. (This type of bonding is known as covalent bonding.) The germanium atom in the center has contributed four electrons to the bonding, one to each bond pair. Figure 3.6B shows the germanium lattice with an arsenic atom replacing one germanium atom. Arsenic has five electrons available for bonding; the germanium lattice will accept only four of those electrons. The extra electron is available for conduction, since it is not involved in any bond-

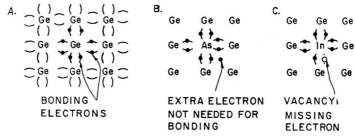

Fig. 3.6. A: Pure material germanium. B: Germanium with arsenic doping. C: Germanium with indium doping.

ing process. The arsenic has donated a conduction electron and is known as a *donor* atom. The drawing in Fig. 3.6C shows a similar situation with indium as the impurity atom. Indium has only three electrons available for bonding; thus, one of four pairs of bonds will have a deficiency of electrons, and a hole has been created. The impurity is said to have accepted a valence electron from the germanium and is called an *acceptor*.

Note that doped semiconductor materials are still electrically neutral. The donor atoms inserted into the semiconductor lattice have as many protons in their nuclei as electrons in their electron clouds. In the acceptor case, the acceptor atom has one less electron than the host and also one less proton in its nucleus than the host atoms have. Consequently, there are no unbalanced charges in doped materials. The difference is that there are more conduction electrons or unfilled hole states in the doped materials than in the pure semiconductors.

Semiconductor materials doped with donor impurities have an excess of conduction electrons. Thus, when an electric field is applied, the principal component of current flow is electron flow. This material is called *n*-type, since the principal carriers of current are negative. Semiconductors doped with acceptor impurities have an excess of holes. The principal carriers of current are positive, and the material is said to be *p*-type. Note that the carrier concentrations are not dependent on temperature but rather on dopant concentration, which is controlled during the manufacturing process. Therefore the current-carrying capabilities of doped semiconductor materials are characteristically much less temperature dependent than those of pure materials.

3.3.2 Semiconductor Junctions

Although semiconducting materials are interesting in their own right, by far the most interest in these materials is in device applications using semiconducting junctions. In fact, the basis for the extensive transistor technology is the behavior of electrons and holes at a junction between two dissimilar materials, one *p*-type and the other *n*-type. Before we discuss transistors per se, let us examine such a junction.

Semiconducting junctions may be prepared by doping one end of a pure semiconducting crystal with an *n*-type impurity and the other end with a *p*-type material during the growth of the crystal. The center of the crystal contains the junction region between *n*-type and *p*-type materials. In the junction region itself, some of the conduction electrons and holes are redistributed by two processes, diffusion and drift.

Diffusion is the motion of charge due to thermal energy. As noted, since room temperature is actually quite hot when compared to the absolute zero of temperature, the electrons have considerable thermal energy. Some in the *n*-type material near the junction have sufficient energy to diffuse across the junction into the *p*-type material. There these free electrons fill the vacant (hole) states. In addition, because the electrons have left the *n*-region, there are now new hole states in the *n*-region, just as if the holes had themselves diffused from *p*-type to *n*-type material. This charge flow, due to thermal energy, is called the diffusion current. The result is that there is a net positive charge in the *n*-region (which has lost electrons) and a net negative charge in the *p*-region (which has gained electrons).

The *drift* current flows opposite to the diffusion current and is due to the newly formed charge separation just discussed. Because the *p*-region now is negative and the *n*-region is positive, those electrons that diffused over to the *p*-region are now electrically attracted back to the *n*-region. [The thermal energy causes the electrons to cross the boundary (diffusion), and the electric field created by their crossing the boundary pulls them back (drift).] The result is that a dynamic *equilibrium*, which depends on temperature, is set up with some electrons flowing from *n* to *p* and others from *p* to *n*. The higher the temperature, the more energy the electrons have, and the greater the number of electrons flowing across the barrier. The junction region where this process occurs is called the *space charge region* (see Fig. 3.7). It is the key to the usefulness of semiconducting devices, as we now investigate.

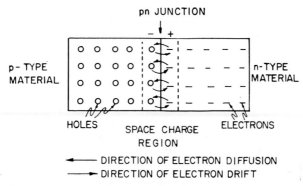

Fig. 3.7. Diffusion and drift of electrons at *pn* junction.

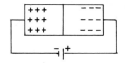

Fig. 3.8.   Reverse-biased *pn* junction.

Suppose we connect a battery as shown in Fig. 3.8, with the positive terminal connected to the *n*-type material and the negative terminal to the *p*-type end. The electric field set up by the battery causes the free electrons in the *n*-type material to be attracted to the positive terminal of the battery and therefore to be pulled away from the space charge junction region. Also, the negative terminal of the battery effectively pulls the holes away from the junction. The resulting situation, shown in Fig. 3.8, is that no charge carriers are near the junction and no current flows. This wiring configuration is *reverse biased.*

In Fig. 3.9 a *forward-biased* junction is shown. This wiring configuration does conduct current. The free electrons in the *n*-type material are driven across the junction by the electric field from the negative terminal of the battery and fill hole states; and conduction continues via hole current as discussed in Section 3.3.1. The battery immediately resupplies electrons to the *n*-side so the total effect is that electrons are flowing. Another way to consider the same picture is to think of the holes as flowing, repelled by the positive terminal of the battery. Either picture is appropriate at the junction. However, since it is useful to describe electron flow through the battery, we normally speak of electron flow through the junction as well.

The device we have discussed is a *diode,* since it conducts when forward biased and does not conduct when reverse biased. Its circuit symbol is shown in Fig. 3.10, where the junction diode is being used as a rectifier. (Compare the junction diode rectifier with the tube diode rectifier in Section 3.2).

3.3.3   Bipolar Transistors

The device that we normally call a transistor is composed of three layers of semiconducting materials, each with its own dopant level, as shown in Fig. 3.11. The ends of the device are of the same materials although they are usually of different dopant levels. The center region,

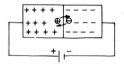

Fig. 3.9.   Forward-biased *pn* junction.

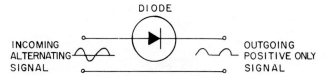

Fig. 3.10. Circuit employing semiconducting junction device as rectifier. Arrowhead in circuit symbol indicates direction positive charges flow through device; electrons always flow opposite to arrow.

called the base, is of a dissimilar material. The result is a device having two *pn* junctions back to back. The *npn* and *pnp* transistors are in principle equivalent (except for a change of polarity in the external circuit), and thus it is sufficient to discuss only the *npn* type.

Consider Fig. 3.12, an illustration of the *npn* bipolar transistor in normal use. We see that the transistor forms a sort of connection between two rather independent circuits. The left side of the drawing shows a complete circuit with a battery and the input signal is fed into the emitter-base junction—the emitter-base junction is forward biased. Current flows in the emitter-base circuit because the junction is forward biased; furthermore, the current has a magnitude that varies with the voltage of the input signal. In itself this varying current flow is not of value. However, the flow of current in the left half (emitter-base circuit) influences the current in the right half (base-collector circuit).

The collector-base circuit in Fig. 3.12 is reverse biased; when no current flows in the emitter-base circuit, no current flows in the collector-base circuit. However, in the normal construction of transistors, the base layer is made so thin that when current flows from the *emitter* to the *base* (forward biased), most of those electrons drift through the thin base into the *collector* region. (With present technology the base may be

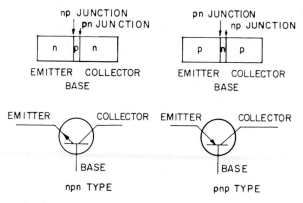

Fig. 3.11. Diagrammatic and circuit representations for *npn* and *pnp* bipolar transistors. Upper drawing indicates "sandwich" stacking of materials; lower drawing shows circuit symbols.

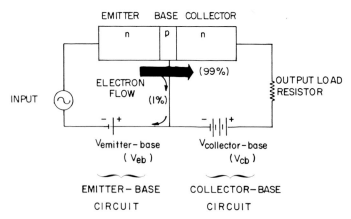

Fig. 3.12. An *npn* bipolar transistor used as amplifier. Emitter-base junction is forward biased by battery V_{eb}; collector-base junction is reverse biased by battery V_{cb}. Symbol used for input indicates that input device is effectively an AC voltage source.

made so thin that as much as 99.9% of the electrons emitted by the emitter pass through the base and into the collector.) Once across the base-collector junction the electrons flow back to the battery through the load resistance. The current in this collector-base circuit varies as the input voltage, because the current across the emitter-base junction varies as the input voltage.

The bipolar transistor circuit shown in Fig. 3.12 is called a common-base circuit, since the base is used in both the input and output circuits. In this wiring configuration the transistor is used as a voltage amplifier. There is no current gain since all the current in the collector circuit also passes through the emitter circuit. However, the voltage in the collector circuit is higher since the voltage supply V_{cb} is larger than V_{eb}. A power amplification is present as well as a voltage amplification, since power equals voltage times current.

Another method of connecting a bipolar transistor into a circuit can provide both current gain and voltage gain, thereby producing very large power amplification. In Fig. 3.13 a common-emitter circuit is shown. As before, the input signal is applied to the forward-biased base-emitter junction. Because battery V_{ce} has a greater potential difference than battery V_{be}, the base is negative with respect to the collector, making the base-collector junction reverse biased. Electrons flow from the emitter to the base and on through to the collector as before. However, note that a very small percentage of the electrons pass through the input branch of the circuit while a much larger percentage (99 times greater) passes through the output branch of the circuit. Therefore, this configuration has produced current amplification as well as the voltage gain of battery V_{ce} over battery V_{be}. The result is a very large power gain, perhaps tens of thousands times greater than the input power.

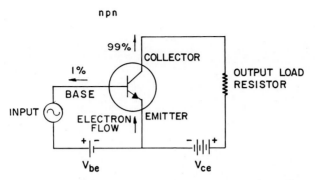

Fig. 3.13.   Bipolar transistor wired in common-emitter configuration.

The drawings of Figs. 3.12 and 3.13 show only two of the simplest ways to use the most basic transistor device. Present technology has advanced so that now entire circuits with many bipolar junction transistors are produced on a single "chip" of semiconducting material. These devices, called integrated circuits, may be smaller than the single transistor of a few years ago. Furthermore, these complete-circuit devices may be reliably mass produced so that the final cost per unit is lower than the cost of a single tube of a few years ago.

As the original bipolar transistor brought in an age of reduction in equipment size, the integrated circuit ushered in the age of miniaturization. Since one integrated circuit chip may contain hundreds or thousands of bipolar junction transistors, all the electronic components for equipment (such as hearing aid amplifiers or pocket calculators) may be made smaller than this typed letter o. The physical size of a pocket calculator is determined by the batteries, the keyboard, and the display, *not* by the electronics. Figure 3.14 shows a $21\times$ magnification of a chip produced for the computer industry. This single unit will operate on as many as sixteen different numbers with simple arithmetic operations as well as perform a host of other convenient computer usages. The relative size of the chip is shown in Fig. 3.15.

The development of circuits using integrated-device technology is beyond the scope of this book. The reader is encouraged to investigate the subject further by examining the materials in the reading list, visiting electronic supply stores carrying resource books, and asking questions of persons knowledgeable in electronics.

3.3.4   Field-Effect Transistors (FETs)

One particular type of solid state device operates with principles similar to those describing vacuum tubes. Recall that in a triode vacuum tube the magnitude of the charge on the grid controls the flow of electrons from the filament to the plate; that is, the grid charge produces an electric field that either enhances (allows more current to flow) or counteracts (retards current flow) the electric field between the

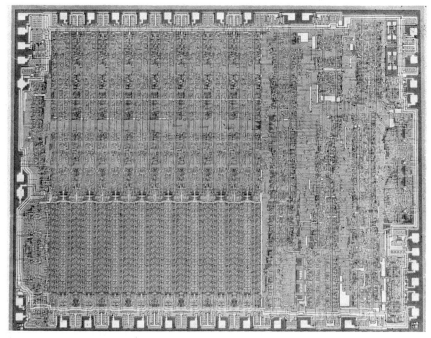

Fig. 3.14.   Enlargement (magnification 21×) of single integrated circuit; device is computer "microprocessor." (Photograph courtesy RCA.)

filament and the plate. In the field-effect transistor (FET) a similar control field is employed.

Consider Fig. 3.16, which shows an FET, the metal-oxide-semiconductor field-effect transistor (MOSFET). Although complicated in appearance, the MOSFET is quite simple to visualize. Electron flow is from the *source* through the channel to the *drain,* just as flow in a vacuum tube is from filament to plate. Here, however, no heat is involved; the *n*-type channel provides a conducting path between the source and drain terminals. The interesting effect involves the amount of current that flows through the channel.

Let us examine the electron flow. In the normal usage of the *n*-type MOSFET, the source is at a negative potential and the drain at a positive potential. The state of the system is "on" with electrons flowing from source to drain. The amount of this electron flow depends on the voltage applied to the source and the drain; on the manufactured characteristics of the conducting channel such as semiconducting dopant level, channel width, depth, and length; and on the temperature.

In addition to the source-channel-drain system, there is also an

Fig. 3.15. Photograph of person holding integrated circuit of type shown in Fig. 3.14. This chip is quite large in comparison with those commonly used in audio applications. (Photograph courtesy RCA.)

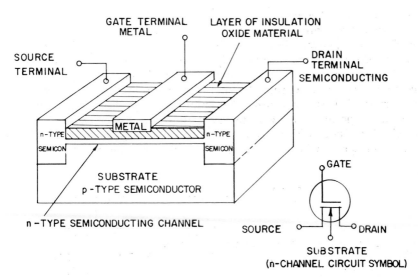

Fig. 3.16. Metal-oxide-semiconductor field-effect transistor (MOSFET), *n*-channel. (All polarity indications would be reversed for *p*-channel MOSFET.)

oxide insulating layer and a metal terminal called the *gate*. By applying a bias voltage to the gate, we can control the effective width of the conducting channel and therefore control the flow of electrons from source to drain. This control is accomplished because any charge on the gate sets up an electric field that penetrates the insulating barrier and influences the charges in the channel. The gate signal can either cause depletion or enrichment of the number of charge carriers in the channel. For a MOSFET with an *n*-type channel as shown in the figure, a negative charge on the gate will reduce conduction by depleting the electron concentration in the channel. A positive charge on the gate will increase the conduction by enriching the electron concentration.

We may think of the gate as a valve controlling the "size" of a pipe through which water is flowing. A positive signal increases the size of the pipe (forward biasing) and allows much water to pass through; a negative signal reduces the size of pipe (reverse biasing) and limits the flow of water (see Fig. 3.17).

The FET provides the simplicity of operation of a vacuum tube as well as the rugged, no-heat characteristics of transistors. ✕ ✕ ✕

3.4   CONTROL OF OUTPUT OF AMPLIFIER

In Sections 3.2 and 3.3 we discuss possible means of amplifying the power in a signal with vacuum tube and transistorized amplifiers. No mention has been made of control of this amplification, such as uniformly increasing or decreasing the amplitude (volume) of the signal, or of control of the amplitude of certain frequency ranges (tone control).

3.4.1   Volume Control

Suppose an amplifier is used to drive a loudspeaker. (We have not yet discussed speakers, but we know a loudspeaker is a device that can convert electrical signals produced by the amplifier into acoustical signals.) Furthermore, suppose the output sound is too loud. How can we reduce the power sent from the amplifier to the loudspeaker? One possible method does not control the amplifier at all but rather controls how much power is allowed to reach the loudspeaker. Consider Fig. 3.18A. A resistor, which dissipates electrical energy as heat, has been placed in series with the loudspeaker. Because the resistor expends

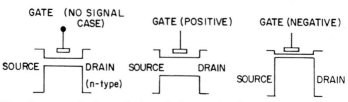

Fig. 3.17.   Conceptual view of size of the conducting channel, controlled by signal, on gate.

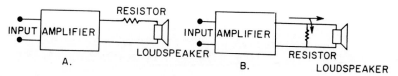

Fig. 3.18. Possible ways of reducing power delivered to loudspeaker. A: Resistor placed in series with speaker. B: Resistor placed in parallel with speaker.

some of the available energy, less power is delivered to the loudspeaker. Figure 3.18B shows a resistor placed in parallel with the loudspeaker. The arrows indicate that some current flowing away from the amplifier is diverted through the resistor, which dissipates the energy carried by that current as heat. Again less power is delivered to the loudspeaker.

The resistors in the above examples could be made to have a *variable* amount of electrical resistance. By controlling the amount of resistance we could change the amount of power delivered to the loudspeakers and thereby control the volume of the sound produced. To understand how we might make a variable resistor, consider Fig. 3.19. Between the points marked A and B is a wire of length L that has resistance. The arrow represents a contact that touches the resistance wire at a distance l from point A. Suppose this device is connected to an external circuit such that an electron current flows from the terminal marked IN through the resistance wire down to the arrow contact and through the terminal marked OUT. The amount of resistance seen by the electrons depends on where the contact touches the resistance wire. If l is 1 cm, the resistance will be a particular amount; if l is 2 cm, the resistance will be twice that amount. By determining where the contact touches the wire, we control the amount of resistance between the IN and OUT terminals. In practice the resistance wire is usually coiled around a ring, and the contact is rotated by a knob. This type of variable resistance is called a *potentiometer*.

The above is a possible way of controlling volume, but it is essentially never used as volume control in a real circuit. At least two reasons why one does not control volume at the output are (1) much of the power output of the amplifier would be lost as heat to the resistor and (more important) (2) the combination of the variable resistor and loudspeaker would present a "variable load" to the amplifier. In Chapter 4

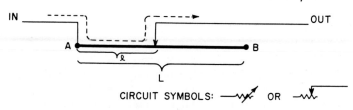

Fig. 3.19. Diagram of means of creating variable resistance.

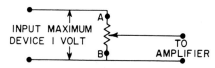

Fig. 3.20. Potentiometer used as voltage divider to determine maximum input levels to amplifier.

on impedance matching we discuss how a load affects the signal brought into it. For now it is sufficient to point out that the variable properties of volume control at the ouput stage are undesirable. ←──── ✳✳✳

The common way of controlling volume is to control the voltage at an input stage to an amplifier or some intermediate stage. You may have noticed that in most component stereo systems the volume control is on the preamplifier stage. This method prevents the amplifier loading problems mentioned previously and virtually eliminates wasted power by working with low power signals.

An example of such a method is shown in Fig. 3.20 where a simple potentiometer serves as the connecting (and controlling) link between an input device such as a phonograph turntable and an amplifier. The slide contact and one end are connected to the amplifier. Suppose the input device generates a maximum voltage of 1 V. By sliding the contact, the maximum voltage fed to the amplifier may be controlled to be any value between zero and 1 V. If the amplifier is designed to cause a voltage gain of 100, then the maximum output voltage will vary between zero and 100 V, depending on the setting of the potentiometer. →Thus we have controlled the output of the amplifier by controlling the input signal level. ←────

3.4.2 Tone Controls
✳✳✳ → [By using tone controls we can alter the frequency response of an amplifier to suit personal tastes or particular listening needs.] For example, if a certain listening room contains heavy drapes, thick carpet, and upholstered furniture, high frequency sounds from a sound-producing system may be severely attenuated by room absorption. (See Backus, [1969] for discussion of absorption.) It may be necessary to boost the amplification of high frequency sounds to a higher level than that of low frequencies to produce equal intensities of all frequencies for the listener.

Furthermore, for low intensity sounds we must boost the amplification of both low and high frequencies above midrange frequencies (around 300 Hz) because of a characteristic of human hearing. One reason for this characteristic is that our eardrums are at the rear of an approximately 1-in auditory canal. This channel acts as a resonant chamber, and because of the canal size and shape, resonates sounds of frequency of about 3000 Hz. Thus, at low intensity it is much easier for humans to hear at midrange frequencies than at either the high or low ends of the audible frequency spectrum. Another reason for this variation in sensitivity is that the ear mechanism is too stiff at low frequencies to vibrate freely and too massive at high frequencies. The results of both effects are shown in Fig. 3.21 on a graph showing the Fletcher-Munson curves.

The frequency response of an amplifier can be controlled by several practical methods. We shall discuss a simplified technique because of its basic physical approach. (This method is not often employed in commercial equipment.) Our approach involves filtering out certain frequencies. To understand how frequencies may be filtered, we must understand further the properties of capacitors consisting of two plates separated by some insulating material (air, paper, plastic, etc.). In Fig. 3.22, a schematic drawing of a capacitor connected to a battery is shown. Initially the switch is open and no electrons flow (A). Suppose we close the switch. Immediately current flows (B), building up an excess of electrons on the left plate of the capacitor and creating a positive (electron-deficient) charge on the right plate. The ammeter

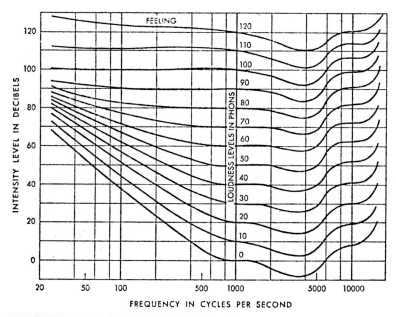

Fig. 3.21. Fletcher-Munson curves. Each contour represents sounds perceived to be equally loud by average adults. For example, two sounds, one of frequency 3000 Hz and intensity 15 dB and the other of frequency 40 Hz and intensity 68 dB, are perceived as equally loud. Units on center vertical axis (phons) are used as measure of loudness. (From P. B. Denes and E. N. Pinson, *The Speech Chain,* p. 82; © 1963, Bell Telephone Lab., Inc. Used by permission.)

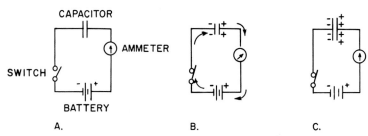

Fig. 3.22.   Flow of electrons in capacitive circuit with direct current.

senses this electron flow and shows a deflection. Soon, however, the charge buildup on the capacitor is sufficient to repel any further electron flow, and the current stops. From that time on, no electrons flow and the ammeter shows no deflection (C). From this analysis we conclude that after an initial buildup of charge, direct current (as provided by a battery) does not pass through a capacitor.

Alternating current does "pass through" a capacitor. Figure 3.23 shows the same arrangement as before with an alternating voltage source (A). Suppose we close the switch at an instant when the left side of the alternating voltage source is negative with respect to the right side, just as the battery was in the previous discussion. Electrons will flow to the left plate, the right plate will become positive, and the ammeter will indicate current flow (B). Before the capacitor can reach full charge, the alternating voltage will change its polarity (C). Thus, the current will reverse, electrons will flow out of the left side of the capacitor leaving it positive, and the ammeter will deflect to the opposite side indicating a reversed direction of electron flow. Because the voltage source continues to alternate in polarity, the current flow continues periodically reversing in direction. The alternating deflection of the ammeter shows that alternating current appears to "pass through" the capacitor.

Consider that a voltage signal in an amplifier is simply an alternating voltage. Low frequencies have relatively long periods of time between alternations of polarity; high frequencies have rather short times. Because of the time difference, low frequencies behave more like

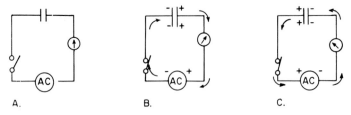

Fig. 3.23.   Flow of electrons in capacitive circuit with alternating current.

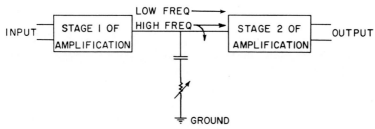

Fig. 3.24. Circuit to boost bass by filtering out some of high frequency signal. (Adapted from *Solid-State Devices Manual SC-16,* 1975, RCA, p. 306. Used by permission.)

direct current than do high frequencies; that is, a given capacitor will "pass" high frequency signals more efficiently than low frequency signals.

In Fig. 3.24 we use this feature to create a bass boost by filtering out some of the high frequency signal. The capacitor passes high frequencies through the resistor to ground. A signal starting from the first stage of amplification with equal-voltage low and high frequency components will enter the second stage of amplification with higher voltage for the low frequency signal, and the result appears to be a bass boost.◄

An effective boost of treble (high frequency) components of a signal may be done in a similar manner: selective attenuation of low frequencies. Figure 3.25 shows a circuit in which a capacitor is used to pass high frequency signals directly to a second stage of amplification. The low frequency components, however, are not efficiently passed by the capacitor and must pass through the resistor. The resistor attenuates all signals passing through it. The result is a reduction in the voltage of low frequency components relative to the voltage of the high frequency components of the signal, effectively boosting the treble. ◄——

The above filters may be described as passive: they do nothing to increase the signal. [Most tone controls presently used are active elements that actually do boost certain frequencies rather than reduce other frequencies.] With these active elements we may either boost or cut a particular region of the frequency spectrum without disturbing the remainder of the spectrum. Devices called spectrum equalizers are available that divide the audible spectrum into several frequency chan-

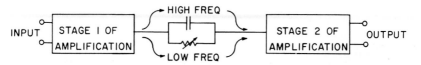

Fig. 3.25. Circuit to increase treble by attenuating bass. (Adapted from *Solid-State Devices Manual SC-16,* 1975, RCA, p. 304. Used by permission.)

nels and allow the user to boost or cut the frequencies in each channel independently.

Finally, many commercial amplifiers have controls identified as loudness compensation controls or simply loudness switches. These devices are not intended to serve a volume control function but rather are used to adjust the frequency response of the amplifier to agree with the Fletcher-Munson curves in Fig. 3.21. [When the loudness switch is on, the response of the amplifier is adjusted such that bass and treble frequencies are boosted without disturbing midrange frequencies. The result is that even at low volume levels, bass frequencies may be heard.] *

3.5   DISTORTION IN AMPLIFIERS

We shall not discuss in detail the origin of distortion in amplifiers but rather shall identify different types of distortion. *Harmonic distortion* is the creation of new harmonic frequencies by an amplifier. For example, suppose the input signal is of frequency f_0. Possibly the amplifier may create new components of the signal with frequencies $2f_0$, $3f_0$, etc., which are the simple multiples or harmonics of the input signal. The output signal is therefore different from the input signal, and distortion has resulted.

Intermodulation distortion is perhaps more important to the listener. Suppose the input signal consists of two frequencies, f_0 and f_1. An ideal amplifier would simply boost the power of both signals. However, in practical amplifiers the two input frequencies will interact with each other. The result will be new signals $(f_0 + f_1)$ and $(f_0 - f_1)$ created by amplifier intermodulation distortion. The final output is again different from the input.

Clipping is the form of distortion that results when the input signal is of such large amplitude that the amplifier power is not sufficient to boost the signal by the appropriate gain factor. For example, suppose the gain controls are set to produce a power gain of 60 dB, which is no problem for small signals. However, percussive instruments, such as pianos, create large amplitude signals on the initial impact of the hammer with the string, even when played relatively softly. For the amplifier to boost these strong signals by 60 dB may require more available output power than the amplifier has. A maximum current and a maximum voltage are available to the output tubes or transistors, and thus the maximum power is limited.) For these large signals the output power increases to the maximum available power and then saturates at that value. Figure 3.26 shows that the output signal appears to be clipped.

3.6   HEAT IN AMPLIFIERS

Those of us who have purchased audio amplifiers will remember reading a warning in the instruction manual about keeping the unit in an area with free airflow. Such a caution is very important; in tube units the heat is often great enough to melt wiring, and in transistorized

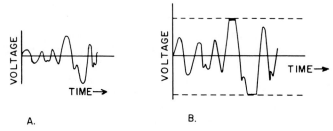

Fig. 3.26. Voltage signal before (A) and after (B) amplification. Dashed lines indicate maximum output voltage of amplifier.

systems the heat will destroy the transistors themselves and melt chassis solder connections. [In fact, the greatest single cause of amplifier failure is damage due to overheating.] ◄— ✶ ✶ ✶ ✶

We have touched on what heat is: thermal energy, expressed as motion of the atoms and molecules in a body. The higher the temperature, the higher the average energy of the particles. In fact, temperature is a measure of the average energy of particles in a body. With these points in mind, let us examine how we can remove heat from an amplifier to keep it cool.

The three methods of heat transfer are: conduction, convection, and radiation. All three have some importance in amplifier cooling.

Conduction is the heat transfer of two objects in contact with each other. The heat flow is simple: the molecules of the hotter object bounce against the molecules of the colder object and transfer heat by collision. If nothing else happens, the two objects will eventually reach the same temperature.

Often, on transistorized amplifiers, one will see that the output transistors are firmly attached to large, metal "heat sinks." Here conduction is used for heat removal: as the transistor gets hot, the case of the transistor heats, and the heat is transferred to the large heat sink. Normally a second stage of conduction then occurs as the air in contact with the heat sink removes heat from the metal. (Often heat sinks have fins to increase the surface area in contact with the air.)

We can understand how each of these processes contributes to the cooling by examining the following equation that describes heat flow by conduction along a body:

$$\frac{\text{heat}}{\text{time}} = \frac{KA}{l}\,(\Delta T) \tag{3.2}$$

This equation states that the amount of heat (measured in joules or calories) that flows per unit time depends on: K, the *thermal conductivity* of the body (similar to electrical conductivity); A, the cross-sectional area of the body; l, the length of the body; and ΔT, the difference in temperature between the two ends. A good conductor (large value of K) such as copper or aluminum conducts heat well. The larger the cross-sectional area A, the more heat can flow per unit time. A large temperature difference causes increased heat flow. The longer the distance l between the ends, the lower the heat flow. Consequently, heat sinks are usually made of aluminum and have very large surface areas to encourage the transfer of heat to the air.

After the exchange of heat from sink to air, *convection* occurs. Convection is the flow of heat due to the motion of the air (or other fluid). As air is heated it expands, creating a lower density in the heated region. The surrounding air (cooler, higher density) then pushes the warm air up. We say hot air rises but actually it is pushed up just as a helium (or hot-air) balloon is pushed up because it has less mass than the surrounding air. The less dense material "floats" on the more dense material. This rising warm air sets up a flow of air, a breeze, that continually flows by the fins of the heat sink.

Suppose convection did not occur, as would happen if an amplifier were covered or boxed in. Then the air in contact with the fins of the heat sink would stay at the heat sink. Air has a low conductivity K, so the heat would build up, and the fins and air would become hotter and hotter. Result: no cooling, even though conduction is working properly.

If convection is allowed to take place by allowing free airflow around the amplifier, the air in contact with the fins heats and rises and is replaced by cool air. Thus, the fins are continually being cooled and the amplifier is protected. (If it is necessary to enclose an amplifier in a cabinet, install a blower fan to provide circulating air.)

The third method of heat transfer, *radiation,* is not quite so important for amplifier cooling, but is interesting in its own right. Radiation is the process of converting heat (thermal motion) in a body into (predominately) infrared waves that radiate like visible light waves. We humans have infrared sensors (nerves) in our skin. If we walk near a hot object, we know it is hot by sensing the infrared radiation. We cannot see infrared radiation, but we can feel it.

The amount of heat given off a body by radiation depends on the temperature of the body. In fact, the amount of heat radiated per second away from a body depends on the fourth power (T^4) of the absolute temperature of the body. If the absolute temperature of a body is doubled, the amount of heat radiated per second will be sixteen times greater ($2^4 = 16$)!

One aspect of radiation cooling can be exploited for audio purposes. The heat radiated per second also depends on the surface radiating heat. A polished, silvery surface does not radiate well. A flat black surface radiates best of all. Thus, flat black, anodized heat sinks lose heat by radiation better than polished, silvery surfaces and thereby offer more efficient cooling.

3.7 SUMMARY

(1) The purpose of amplification in most audio applications is to increase the *power* of a signal. Instantaneous power in a signal is given by

$$P = IV \tag{3.1}$$

(2) Transformers may change the voltage and current in a signal but do not change the power of the signal.

(3) Vacuum tubes contain elements called filament, grid, and plate. Electrons are boiled off the filament by heat and flow to the plate which is positively charged. A voltage signal applied to the grid can control the flow of electrons from the filament to the plate. The triode vacuum tube may be used as an amplifier because a low power signal on the grid can control a high power filament-to-plate current.

(4) Metals are materials for which essentially all electron energy states are allowed. As a result, electrons may change states easily and flow in response to an electric field. Semiconductors are materials that have a small band gap of forbidden electron energy states. Electrons with energy higher than the band gap may contribute to conduction. Vacancies, or hole states, below the band gap may also be thought of as contributing to conduction. Insulators have such large band gaps that essentially no electrons exist with energies higher than the gap.

(5) Doping small amounts of other materials into intrinsic or pure semiconducting materials may be used to increase the concentration of either conduction electrons (in *n*-type materials) or holes (in *p*-type materials).

(6) Junctions between *n*-type and *p*-type materials may be used as rectifiers (or one-way valves) for electron flow. Forward biasing a junction will cause current to flow; reverse biasing will stop current flow.

(7) Bipolar transistors employ two *pn* junctions. The current flow through the forward-biased emitter-base junction causes current flow across the reverse-biased base-collector junction. The transistor may be used as an amplifier because a low power signal in the emitter-base circuit controls a high power signal in the base-collector circuit.

(8) Field-effect transistors are solid-state devices that employ the electric field from a small signal on the gate to control the high power current flowing from source to drain.

(9) Variable resistors may be used to control power in a signal by dissipating part of the signal.

(10) Because capacitors "pass" high frequency signals and resistors "pass" low frequency signals, various combinations of capacitors and resistors may be used to devise tone controls in an audio system.

(11) Any change of a signal other than uniform increasing of power in an amplifier can be called distortion. Generation of harmonics and intermodulation distortion are two of the most likely types of amplifier distortion. Clipping results when an amplifier does not have the necessary power to reproduce a large signal.

(12) Three types of heat transfer are: conduction, which depends

on contact; convection, which depends on air (or fluid) flow; and radiation of infrared waves.

QUESTIONS

1. What is power? Do power companies (which charge by the kilowatt-hour) sell power or energy?
2. Thermionic emission of electrons from a hot cathode in a vacuum tube has been described as "boiling off" electrons. Try to compare thermionic emission to the escape of water molecules in boiling water.
3. Why will electrons only flow one way in a vacuum tube?
4. What is the fundamental difference between a metal and a semiductor?
5. How can one dope germanium with arsenic to produce an n-type semiconductor material and still have the final product be electrically neutral (uncharged)?
6. Describe the difference between the diffusion current and the drift current at a pn junction.
7. Explain what is meant by forward biasing a pn junction.
8. In Fig. 3.25 the high frequency components are shown as primarily routed through the capacitor and the low frequency components primarily routed through the resistor. Justify this routing.
9. In Exercise 16 of Chapter 1 it takes a tenfold increase in amplifier power to make a sound seem "twice as loud." Explain why clipping is a much stronger argument for buying high power equipment than the argument for making "louder" sounds.

EXERCISES

1. An ideal transformer with twice as many turns on the primary as on the secondary windings has a signal with a peak voltage of 100 V applied to it. What will be the peak voltage across the secondary windings? (Answer: 50 V)
2. An ideal transformer known to convert 75-V (peak) signals into 150-V (peak) signals has 2000 turns of wire on the primary. How many turns make up the secondary winding?
3. An ideal transformer converts a signal with peak characteristics 100 V and 2 A to a signal with peak voltage 1000 V. What is the peak current of the new signal?
4. A bipolar transistor is wired in a common-emitter configuration as shown in Fig. 3.13. It is found that the input (base-emitter) circuit carries 0.001 A (1 mA) and $V_{be} = 0.1$ V. The output circuit is measured to carry 0.1 A for the battery $V_{ce} = 20$ V. What is the power gain of the system? (Answer: $P_o/P_i = 2 \times 10^4$)
5. A voltage divider (Fig. 3.20) is constructed from a variable resistor of maximum resistance 100,000 Ω. An input voltage of 20 V is applied. If the movable contact of the variable resistor is set precisely at the center of resistor windings, what will be the output voltage?

4

IMPEDANCE

Throughout the preceding chapters we have discussed connecting stages of amplifiers to each other or connecting microphones into amplifiers, etc. We have not considered one very important topic concerning the interconnection between two components: impedance matching.

Impedance is the name of the property of an electrical circuit that resists the flow of alternating current just as resistance resists the flow of direct current. Because all audio signals involve alternating (that is, periodically varying) voltages or current, impedance is an important subject for us to investigate.

The concept of impedance, however, is more general than the impedance of electric circuits. For example, a mechanical system responds to an external driving force in a manner determined by *mechanical impedance*. The behavior of a sound wave in a large room is determined by *acoustical impedance*. Because mechanical systems are somewhat easier to visualize than electrical or acoustical systems, we will begin our discussion with a mechanical system—a microphone.

4.1 MECHANICAL IMPEDANCE

Suppose we have an open, free diaphragm suspended by springs as shown in Fig. 4.1. Furthermore, let us assume that the diaphragm is in a vacuum; there is no air resistance. If we push the diaphragm to the right and release it, it will oscillate back and forth with some frequency f_0, the characteristic resonant frequency of the system. You may recall from Chapter 1 that the resonant frequency depends on the spring constant k and the mass of the diaphragm m: $f_0 = (1/2\pi) \sqrt{k/m}$. Now we allow some air into the region so that the diaphragm has to push against the air in order to vibrate. The new frequency of free vibration will be lower than before, but the motion will still be periodic. Next, we allow a sound wave to travel through the air and cause the diaphragm to move. The sound wave applies a periodic driving force to the diaphragm. The diaphragm will oscillate back and forth with the same frequency as that of the driving force. However, there are two differences of this driven motion from the free motion when no force was applied. These differ-

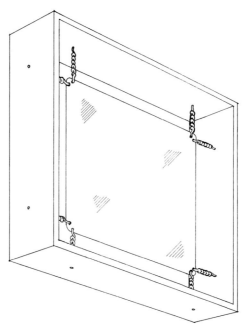

Fig. 4.1. Movable diaphragm supported by springs attached to rigid frame.

ences are (1) the *amplitude* and (2) the *phase* of the motion of the diaphragm, which depend on the frequency of the driving force.

Consider first the amplitude. Recalling that the natural frequency
of vibration of the free system is f_0, suppose we try to drive the diaphragm
back and forth with a frequency a hundred times greater, $f = 100\, f_0$. The
diaphragm would hardly move at all; the system just does not oscillate
well at such high frequencies because of the mass of the diaphragm. On
the other hand, if we use a driving frequency equal to the natural frequency, resonance would occur and the system would oscillate through
very large amplitude. For a driving frequency lower than the natural frequency, the system will respond with amplitude much lower than that of
the resonance case. Representative plots of amplitude versus driving frequency are shown in Fig. 4.2.

Note that the height and width of the resonant peak are quite different for the various plots. These differences depend on several properties of the system, but the chief determining factor is the mechanical
damping or friction. (Recall our discussion of the need for damping to
smooth the response of ribbon microphones.) The larger the damping,
the broader the peak and the lower the height. Good microphone design
would have sufficient damping to cause the amplitude versus frequency
curve to be almost flat and very broad so that all driving frequencies
would cause essentially the same response in the system.

The second new characteristic of mechanical systems with driving

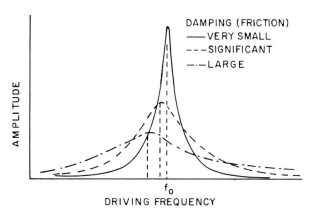

Fig. 4.2. Amplitude of motion of mechanical system responding to external driving force of frequency f; the three cases correspond to different amounts of frictional damping in system.

forces is in the phase of the motion. The actual motion of the diaphragm may lag behind (in time) or even precede the driving force. By this we mean that as the driving force pushes to the right, the system may actually be moving to the left. To illustrate this one may simply push a child on a playground swing. The following will be observed:

(1) When we push with a frequency equal to the natural frequency of the swing, the motion of the swing is exactly *inphase* with the driving force. Our push or pull is always in the same direction as the velocity of the swing. At the end points of the motion both the driving force and the velocity are zero.

(2) When we push with a frequency slower than the natural frequency, we end up just simply pulling the swing along, always pulling on the upswing motion and holding back on the downswing motion. In fact, at the end points of the swing motion, we have to pull to keep the swing from naturally falling back on its own.

(3) When we push with a frequency higher than the natural frequency, the swing seems to us to be always behind in its response. At the end points of the motion where the velocity is zero, we have to push rather than let the swing naturally fall on its own. We are always trying to "speed up the swing" to make it oscillate with a frequency higher than the natural frequency.

These three cases are illustrated in Fig. 4.3.

The result is that the phase of the motion of a mechanical system can lag behind, equal, or precede the phase of the driving force.

We see that some property of a system determines the response to a driving force. That property is called the impedance Z and is defined (for a mechanical system) as

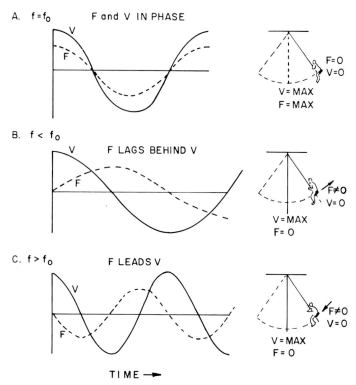

A. f = f₀   F and V IN PHASE

B. f < f₀

C. f > f₀

TIME →

Fig. 4.3. Comparison of velocity and driving force for different driving frequencies.

$$Z = \frac{F}{v} \tag{4.1}$$

where F is the driving force and v is the velocity. The impedance Z is not a number expressed by a simple digit, but rather is what mathematicians call a "complex number." It has two parts, a "real" part and an "imaginary" part. (The meanings of the words "real" and "imaginary" have little to do with the common usage of the terms.) The real and imaginary parts are convenient mathematical ways to describe the amplitude and the phase of a quantity such as impedance.

For an actual mechanical system, the impedance Z is different for different frequencies. At the resonant frequency, Z is entirely real (the imaginary part is zero). For other frequencies Z will be a combination of a real part and an imaginary part. Let us examine the quantities that affect Z: friction, mass, and compliance. "Compliance" is new to us; it is the reciprocal of the spring constant k discussed earlier while examining Hooke's force law for spring systems: $F = -kx$. These three quantities cause the following effects on the mechanical impedance and resulting motion.

(1) *Friction* has three effects on the motion: it lowers the resonant frequency, it reduces the amplitude of the motion at resonance and broadens the resonant peak (as we saw in Fig. 4.2), and it dissipates the energy of the system. If the driving force is removed, the motion will eventually cease as friction slowly converts the mechanical energy of the system into heat.

(2) The *mass* dominates the behavior of the system in response to driving forces of very high frequencies. Furthermore, mass is important in determining the resonant frequency of the system. The larger the mass, the lower the resonant frequency.

(3) The *compliance* $(C = 1/k)$ dominates the response of the system to driving forces of frequency lower than the resonant frequency. Furthermore, the larger the compliance (that is, the weaker the spring constant k), the larger the amplitude of the motion for all frequencies far from the resonant frequency. Lastly, the compliance also is responsible for determining the resonant frequency of the system: the larger the compliance, the lower the resonant frequency.

Later we consider electrical quantities analogous to these mechanical ones.

In conclusion, let us point out that it is rather unusual for students of audio to use mechanical impedance directly. We have introduced it here in order to discuss the concept of impedance rather than to give a thorough treatment of mechanical impedance itself. However, we should realize that the subject itself is of critical importance in the design of audio equipment. For example, the mechanical resonance of a turntable tone arm or of a cone of a loudspeaker is entirely determined by the mechanical impedance of the system. The response of a microphone diaphragm to a sound wave or of a stylus to a groove in a record is determined by the mechanical impedance of the system. These are just a few of the many ways in which mechanical impedance affects the behavior of a sound reproduction system.

4.2 ELECTRICAL IMPEDANCE

Having developed the idea that the impedance of a system determines how that system responds to a driving force, we now examine the response of an electrical circuit to an electrical driving force. In Fig. 4.4 we show such a circuit using the three basic elements: a resistor R, a capacitor C, and a coil L (more properly referred to as an "inductor"). These elements are connected in series with an alternating voltage source V. To determine the response, we wish to measure the voltage and current across each element. In Chapter 6 we examine how such a circuit involving capacitance and inductance (with a very small resistance) can oscillate electrically with a back-and-forth flow of current just as a spring system oscillates mechanically with a back-and-forth motion. For now, let us examine the impedance of this electrical system, assuming that it has oscillating current flow.

Let us consider the three elements one at a time.

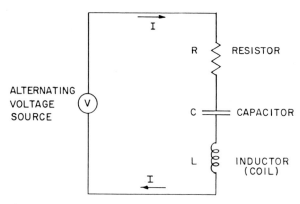

Fig. 4.4. Series circuit containing alternating voltage source, resistance, capacitance, and inductance; current I is indicated for one particular time.

(1) Resistance: We have seen from Ohm's law *(V = IR)* that a resistance R determines the flow of current I when connected to a battery of voltage V. The larger the resistance, the smaller the current. In fact, resistance in an electrical circuit can be compared with friction or damping in a mechanical system. Resistance lowers the resonance frequency of an oscillating system, broadens the resonance curve, and dissipates energy. Furthermore, in a circuit that has only resistance, the current and voltage are exactly inphase with each other.

(2) Capacitance: If we start with an uncharged capacitor and cause current to begin to flow, charge will build up on the plates of the capacitor until the voltage across the capacitor is sufficient to oppose the driving voltage. Then the current will cease. We see that when the current is maximum, the voltage across the capacitor is zero. When the current is zero, the voltage is maximum. Therefore, a capacitor presents an impedance to an electrical circuit that causes the voltage (analogous to the force) to lag behind the current (analogous to the velocity) by one-fourth cycle. Capacitance is similar to the compliance in a mechanical circuit. Capacitance impedes the flow of low frequency alternating current and is one quantity involved in the determination of the resonant frequency. The larger the capacitance, the lower the resonant frequency.

(3) Inductance: What happens when current flows in a coil? Recall that anytime a current flows in a coil, it sets up a magnetic field around the coil. The strength of the magnetic field depends on the number of turns of wire, the size of the coil, etc. These properties are represented by a quantity called the inductance. Creating this field removes energy from the current flow and stores it in the magnetic field. Later, as the current flow decreases (remember that current flow is alternating), the magnetic field begins to collapse and feed its energy back into the system. (The inductance in the electrical circuit can be compared with

the mass in the mechanical system—when a pendulum is on the down-swing, gravitational force on the mass of the pendulum causes the motion to increase in velocity.) A collapsing magnetic field causes a similar response in a coil. The reason the field exists is because current is flowing; if we try to stop the current, the decreasing magnetic field will continue to push electrons through the coil until all the energy stored in the magnetic field has been fed back into the electron flow. The result is that the voltage across an inductor leads the current by one-fourth cycle. The inductance impedes the flow of high frequency signals just as mass impeded high frequency motion. Furthermore, the inductance is important in determining the resonant frequency. The larger the inductance, the lower the resonant frequency.

When these elements are combined in a series circuit as shown in Fig. 4.4, that circuit will have resonant behavior. That is, if we vary the frequency of the alternating driving voltage (force), we shall obtain a maximum current (response) at some particular frequency. Just as the sharpness of the mechanical resonance curves in Fig. 4.2 depends on the damping force, the sharpness of the electrical resonance curves depends on the resistance. Furthermore, just as the phase of mechanical system's response depends on mass and compliance, the phase relationship between current and voltage in an electrical system depends on the inductance and the capacitance.

By analogy with the mechanical system we can write down the resonant frequency of an electrical circuit. In the mechanical system,

$$f_0 = \frac{1}{2\pi} \sqrt{\frac{k}{m}}$$

In the electrical system the inductance L is analogous to the mass m; and the capacitance C is analogous to the compliance $1/k$, the inverse spring constant. Therefore, we can simply replace m by L and k by $1/C$ to give the electrical resonant frequency,

$$f = \frac{1}{2\pi} \sqrt{\frac{1}{LC}} \tag{4.2}$$

We return to this formula in our discussion of radio.

Throughout this discussion we see that the response of an electrical circuit depends on the impedance properties of the circuit. The ratio of voltage V to the current I defines that impedance Z,

$$Z = \frac{V}{I} \tag{4.3}$$

where the voltage and the current may not be inphase with each other.

4.3 IMPEDANCE MATCHING

We have developed some understanding of the property of impedance. Now let us examine some practical situations in which the users of
audio equipment need to be careful about "matching" the impedance of
various components (microphones, amplifiers, speakers, etc.) when connecting them.

First we investigate a simple electrical circuit involving only resistive
elements and a battery. The situation is as follows: we have a source of
power and we wish to transfer that power to a second device such as a
light bulb as shown in Fig. 4.5. We have not previously mentioned the
fact that any source of power such as a battery has its own internal
resistance. In our previous discussions this resistance could be ignored,
but here it cannot. For example, suppose the internal resistance R_s of
the source is 10 Ω (ohms). What should be the resistance of the load for
maximum power transfer?

We can solve this problem by recalling from Eq. (2.3) that when resistors are in series, the total resistance is given by the sum of the individual resistances. Therefore, $R_{total} = R_s + R_{load}$. Furthermore, the current flowing through the entire circuit can be found from Ohm's law (Eq.
2.2): $V_{source} = IR_{total}$, so $I = V/R_{total}$. Then, once we know the current
I flowing through the circuit, we can calculate the power delivered to the
load. We shall use the relation given in Eq. (3.1), $P = IV$, which states
that the power delivered to some component depends on the product of
the current through the component times the voltage drop across the
component, so $P_{load} = IV_{load}$. We know how to·write V_{load} from Ohm's
law: $V_{load} = IR_{load}$. Thus,

$$P = IV_{load} = I(IR_{load}) = I^2R_{load} \qquad (4.4)$$

Let us calculate the power delivered to the load resistor for three
different values of R_{load} when $R_{source} = 10$ Ω and $V = 10$ V (Fig. 4.5).

Case 1. $R_{load} = 1$ Ω $R_s = 10$ Ω $V = 10$ V
      total resistance: $R_{total} = R_s + R_{load} = 10$ Ω $+ 1$ Ω $= \underline{11 \text{ Ω}}$
      current: $I = V/R = 10$ V$/11$ Ω $= \underline{0.9 \text{ A}}$
      power delivered: $P = I^2R_{load} = (0.9 \text{ A})^2(1$ Ω$) = \underline{0.81 \text{ W}}$

Case 2. $R_{load} = 10$ Ω $R_s = 10$ Ω $V = 10$ V
      total resistance: $R_{total} = 10$ Ω $+ 10$ Ω $= \underline{20 \text{ Ω}}$
      current: $I = 10$ V$/20$ Ω $= \underline{0.5 \text{ A}}$
      power delivered: $P = (0.5 \text{ A})^2(10$ Ω$) = \underline{2.5 \text{ W}}$

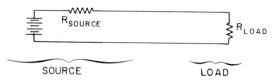

Fig. 4.5. Internal resistance (R_{source}) of battery forms series resistance circuit
with load.

Case 3. $R_{\text{load}} = 100\ \Omega$ $R_s = 10\ \Omega$ $V = 10\ \text{V}$
total resistance: $R_{\text{total}} = 100\ \Omega + 10\ \Omega = \underline{110\ \Omega}$
current: $I = 10\ \text{V}/110\ \Omega = \underline{0.09\ \text{A}}$
power delivered: $P = (0.09\ \text{A})^2(100\ \Omega) = \underline{0.81\ \text{W}}$

We see that maximum power transfer to the load occurs when the resistance of load is "matched" to the resistance of the source (that is, $R_{\text{load}} = R_s$). An even broader statement can be shown to be true: *Maximum power transfer results when the impedances of the source and load are equal.* ⟵——— ✳ ✳ ✳
(This statement can be used as is for buying equipment: be sure impedances match. However, in a detailed analysis of complex number arithmetic, one finds that the maximum power transfer occurs when the real and imaginary parts of the impedances obey

real part: $Z_{\text{source}} = Z_{\text{load}}$
imaginary part: $Z_{\text{source}} = -Z_{\text{load}}$

This subtle, technical detail comes from the condition for resonance and does not concern us here.)

Next, let us investigate connecting a microphone to an amplifier. The manufacturers of both devices state the impedances of the instruments in their literature. Usually audio devices have impedances rated as "low" (around 200 Ω) or "high" (around 10,000 Ω).

Suppose we wish to connect a low impedance microphone into an amplifier that has two different input terminals, one for high impedance and one for low impedance. We will calculate the power transfer from the microphone to the amplifier for each of two possible plug-in cases. (To simplify the calculation, let us assume again that the impedance is purely resistive.) The two cases are sketched in Fig. 4.6. The microphone acts as an alternating voltage generator producing a peak voltage of, say, 0.01 V.

Case 1. $R_{\text{mic}} = 200\ \Omega$ $R_{\text{amp}} = 200\ \Omega$ $V_{\text{max}} = 0.01\ \text{V}$
total resistance: $R_{\text{total}} = R_{\text{mic}} + R_{\text{amp}}$
$= 200\ \Omega + 200\ \Omega = \underline{400\ \Omega}$
current: $I = V/R_{\text{total}} = 0.01\ \text{V}/400\ \Omega = \underline{2.5 \times 10^{-5}\ \text{A}}$
power delivered: $P = I^2 R_{\text{amp}} = (2.5 \times 10^{-5}\ \text{A})^2(200\ \Omega)$
$= (6.25 \times 10^{-10}\ \text{A}^2)(200\ \Omega)$
$= \underline{12.5 \times 10^{-8}\ \text{W}}$

Case 2. $R_{\text{mic}} = 200\ \Omega$ $R_{\text{amp}} = 10,000\ \Omega$ $V_{\text{max}} = 0.01\ \text{V}$
total resistance: $R_{\text{total}} = R_{\text{mic}} + R_{\text{amp}}$
$= 200\ \Omega + 10,000\ \Omega \cong \underline{10^4\ \Omega}$
current: $I = V/R_{\text{total}} = 0.01\ \text{V}/10^4\ \Omega = \underline{10^{-6}\ \text{A}}$
power delivered: $P = I^2 R_{\text{amp}} = (10^{-6}\ \text{A})^2(\underline{10^4\ \Omega})$
$= (10^{-12}\ \text{A}^2)(10^4\ \Omega)$
$= \underline{1 \times 10^{-8}\ \text{W}}$

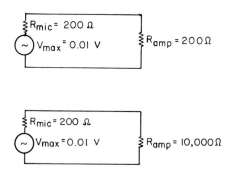

Fig. 4.6. Two cases of low impedance microphone connections to amplifier; microphone is represented by resistor R_{mic} and alternating voltage source and amplifier by its input resistance R_{amp}.

The power delivered to the amplifier is 12 times greater for the proper input connection than for the improper one—simply by connecting the microphone to the wrong input we may cause greater than 10 dB reduction in the audio signal. (This is a common cause of a "weak" microphone. Before blaming the device, check the connections!)

Another place where impedance matching is very important is the connection of an amplifier output to loudspeakers. Two reasons why care should be exercised at this connection are (1) as we have already seen, power transfer to the loudspeakers is maximum when the matched condition exists (a mismatched condition requires the gain of the amplifier to be increased to get the same loudness), and (2) an amplifier can be damaged if its output is not properly matched. ← ———✱ ✱ ✱

To investigate how damage to an amplifier can occur, let us take the worst possible case: the amplifier output terminals are short circuited, which corresponds to no load at all (zero impedance). What will happen? Because the load has no resistance a large current, limited only by the impedance of the amplifier, will flow. Furthermore, no power will be delivered to the load (it has $R = 0$), and thus all the power generated by the amplifier will be expended *in* the amplifier itself. Recall that we pointed out that every source of power has its own internal resistance (impedance). In the case of an output transistor, for example, the resistance is due to the material of which the transistor is made and the construction of the device. The power "expended in the amplifier" would cause severe heating of the transistor as the very large current flowed through it. A possible result is "burning out" the transistor—heating it so much that electronic properties are changed or the lead wires connected to the elements of the transistor are melted. (Many high power amplifiers contain fuses in the output circuit to attempt to alleviate this problem.)

A general rule for connecting speakers to amplifiers is simply to follow the manufacturer's suggestion: check the speaker impedance

(usually 4, 8, or 16 Ω) and connect to the amplifier output terminal ⬅
having the same impedance. | If it is necessary to use a mismatched
system (for example, the amplifier does not have the appropriate terminal), it is better that the amplifier output impedance be *lower than*
the speaker impedance. (Connecting 8-Ω speakers to a 4-Ω output is better than connecting the 8-Ω speakers to a 16-Ω output.) This approach
lowers the possibility of damage to the amplifier.

(We must pause here for a comment to eliminate a misconception
caused by the above discussion: the internal impedance of an amplifier
is *not* equal to the impedance of the load. The internal impedance of
the circuitry at the 8-Ω output is not 8 Ω; it is most likely less than 2
Ω. ⎡The reason is that power transfer is not the only consideration in ⬅ ✱✱✱
driving loudspeakers.⎤ Another important consideration is that loudspeakers, being mechanical systems, tend to overshoot when driven. Recall our discussion of damping of microphones to prevent these same
mechanical problems. Amplifier impedance smaller than speaker impedance produces electrical damping to reduce mechanical problems.
➡ ⎡The ratio of the load impedance to the output impedance is known as
the "damping factor."⎤ This ratio should be 4 or greater for reasonable
damping; some manufacturers even use damping factors of 20 or so. For
a damping factor of 10, the proper amplifier impedance for an 8-Ω load
would be 8 $\Omega/10 = 0.8$ Ω!)

Finally, when connecting combinations of speakers to a single output, one must use care to determine the effective impedance of the combination. Speakers may be treated as parallel or series resistive elements:
in series their impedances add as in Eq. (2.3), and in parallel the total
impedance is

$$\frac{1}{Z_{total}} = \frac{1}{Z_1} + \frac{1}{Z_2} + \cdots \tag{4.5}$$

Thus, if two 8-Ω speakers are connected in parallel (see Fig. 4.7), their
effective total impedance is 4 Ω:

$$\frac{1}{Z_{total}} = \frac{1}{Z_1} + \frac{1}{Z_2} = \frac{1}{8 \ \Omega} + \frac{1}{8 \ \Omega} = \frac{2}{8 \ \Omega}$$

$$\frac{1}{Z_{total}} = \frac{1}{4 \ \Omega} \quad \text{or} \quad Z_{total} = 4 \ \Omega$$

Several books (such as Cohen or Davis and Davis) in the reading
list at the back of the book give helpful suggestions for practical systems
involving combinations of different types of speakers.

In conclusion, let us point out that impedance matching should be
considered at every interconnection in an audio system. Furthermore,

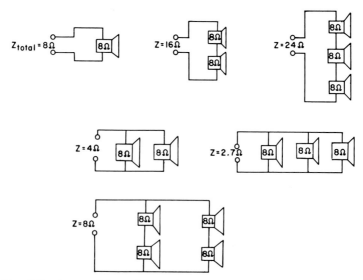

Fig. 4.7. Effective total impedance of one, two, three, and four 8-Ω speakers connected in various arrangements.

before additional purchases are made to "add on" to an existing system, it is wise to investigate compatibility of component impedance matching. The problems at the end of this chapter contain more numerical examples of the importance of impedance matching.

4.4 SUMMARY

(1) Impedance is the property of a system that determines its response to an external driving force. Impedance is measured as the ratio of driving force to response.

(2) In a mechanical system, friction, mass, and compliance (the inverse of the spring constant) determine the impedance.

(3) In an electrical system, resistance, inductance, and capacitance determine the impedance.

(4) Resistance (friction) limits the amplitude of the current (displacement) and broadens the resonant peak when an electrical (mechanical) system is oscillating at resonance.

(5) Inductance (mass) limits the response of an electrical (mechanical) system to driving forces of high frequency and is one factor in determining the resonant frequency.

(6) Capacitance (compliance) limits the response of an electrical (mechanical) system to driving forces of low frequency and is the other chief factor in determining resonant frequency.

(7) Both the amplitude and the phase of the response are de-

termined by impedance because impedance is made up of two parts—a real part and an imaginary part. Such an expression is called a "complex quantity."

(8) At all points in an electrical circuit, components should have matched impedances. The matched condition allows the maximum power transfer between components.

QUESTIONS

1. Define electrical impedance in your own words. Explain how it is different from resistance. In what ways are impedance and resistance similar?
2. What is inductance? How is it analogous to mass?
3. Sketch three current versus frequency plots of an inductance-capacitance-resistance circuit for the cases of small resistance, significant resistance, and very large resistance. Compare your diagram to the figure for response in a mechanical system, Fig. 4.2.
4. To illustrate impedance matching in a mechanical system, think of a long rope with two parts: a heavy, thick piece tied to a light, thin piece. If waves are traveling down the thick rope toward the junction to the thinner piece, what happens when the waves reach the knot? Suppose the waves start on the thin side and travel toward the "impedance mismatch" at the knot; would the wave continue into the thick rope? Would any part of the wave be reflected?
5. What role does resistance play in determining impedance? How does it affect the shape of the resonance curve?
6. What role does capacitance play in determining impedance? How does it affect the resonant frequency?

EXERCISES

1. A current of 0.3 A is flowing through an 8-Ω resistance load. What power is being delivered to the load?
2. A 10-V battery has an internal resistance of 100 Ω. If the battery is connected to a 10-Ω load, how much power is delivered to the load and how much is expended in the battery? Answer the same question for a 100-Ω load. (First answer: 0.08 W)
3. Two 4-Ω speakers are wired in parallel. What is the total impedance of the combination? (Answer: 2 Ω)
4. A 4-Ω speaker and an 8-Ω speaker are wired in parallel. What is the total impedance of the combination?
5. An amplifier rated at 6-W output has output terminals of 4 Ω, 8 Ω, and 16 Ω. These numbers indicate the impedance of the amplifier for each of the terminals. You connect (by mistake) a 16-Ω loudspeaker to the 4-Ω output. If the amplifier produces a voltage of 10 V, how much power is transferred to the speaker? How much power would be transferred if a 4-Ω loudspeaker were attached to the 4-Ω output terminals? (First answer: 4 W)

6. A 6-W amplifier is wired incorrectly with a 4-Ω loudspeaker attached to the 16-Ω output terminals. Calculate the power delivered to the loudspeaker if the output voltage is 25 V. (The 25 V corresponds to the peak voltage that would be generated at the 16-Ω output if the system were properly wired.) Also calculate the power expended inside the amplifier under the same conditions.

5

STORAGE AND RETRIEVAL
OF AUDIO SIGNALS

We have discussed the conversion of audio signals to electrical signals and the amplification of the electrical signals. Next we consider methods of storage and retrieval of the information contained in those signals. Several methods are possible; for example, we can convert the electrical signals to mechanical signals and cut a groove in a plastic record disc. The groove in the disc will contain, as mechanical oscillations, the information of the original audio signals. Another storage method is to convert the electrical signals to variations of a magnetic field and use that field to align magnetic particles on some magnetic material. The final variations of alignment of the particles would contain the original audio information. Or we can convert the electrical signals to varying-intensity light signals and record the light signals by chemical changes on a photographic film. The final variations of dark and light on the film will contain the audio information originally present.

5.1 MECHANICAL STORAGE AND RETRIEVAL FROM DISCS

Just as a magnetic dynamic microphone is able to convert audio (mechanical) signals into electrical signals, another magnetic device can be used to convert electrical signals to mechanical vibrations. In Fig. 5.1 we see a drawing of a device that employs the electrical signal to produce a varying magnetic field in a soft-iron armature to which a sharp cutting tool is attached. If a soft plastic material or a soft metal such as copper is passed beneath the cutting tool, a groove will be cut in the material. As the electrical signal varies from positive to negative, the magnetic field produced in the armature will vary, changing the magnetic polarity in the end of the armature from, say, north to south. When the cutting end of the armature is a north magnetic pole, that end will be repelled by the north pole of the permanent magnet and attracted to the south pole. The cutting tool will swing to the right, rotating about the knife-edge pivot. Thus the groove being cut on the disc will deviate as the cutter swings. Reversing the polarity of the signal again will cause the cutter to swing to the left, and the groove will deviate left. The result is that the electrical variations in the input signal are translated into me-

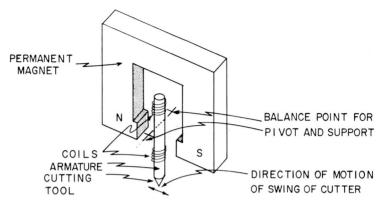

PERMANENT MAGNET

BALANCE POINT FOR PIVOT AND SUPPORT

N

S

COILS
ARMATURE
CUTTING
TOOL

DIRECTION OF MOTION
OF SWING OF CUTTER

Fig. 5.1.   Magnetic cutting head for cutting groove into disc.

chanical vibrations of a cutting tool and "stored" as deviations in the path of a groove on a disc or cylinder, etc. (see Fig. 5.2).

Let us examine how we may retrieve the signal from the groove. One approach would be to attach a sharp-pointed object to another armature around which coils are wound. Suspend the armature in a magnetic field so that when the stylus moves the armature will move in the magnetic field. This motion will induce a changing voltage in the coils, as in the dynamic microphone (see Fig. 5.3A). Or the stylus may be attached to

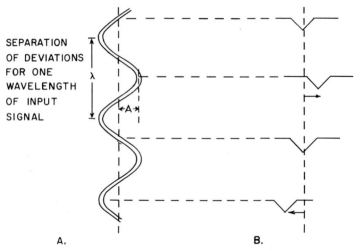

SEPARATION
OF DEVIATIONS
FOR ONE
WAVELENGTH
OF INPUT
SIGNAL

λ

$\leftarrow A \rightarrow$

A.

B.

Fig. 5.2.   Two views of deviations of groove of record in which audio information is stored as lateral vibrations. A: View of groove from above. Signal shown is exaggerated; normal deviations are of order of width of groove. B: Cross-sectional, end-on view of groove for specific points in A; width of cut is amplified for clarity.

the free corner of a piezoelectric crystal so that the motion of the stylus causes bending of the crystal. As in the crystal microphone, this bending produces a voltage across the faces of the crystal by the piezoelectric effect (see Fig. 5.3B). Thus by allowing the stylus of one of these pickup devices to track the groove of a rotating disc, we may extract the audio information in the form of a voltage signal.

5.1.1   Frequency Information on Discs

The lateral deviations of a groove store frequency, by the spacing of the oscillations, and amplitude, by the magnitude of the deviations of the groove. (Additional information is stored, such as the phase of various parts of the signal, sums and differences of more than one signal, etc. We investigate part of this extra information later.) During playback, the disc is rotated with the stylus placed in the recorded groove. Because the groove deviates from side-to-side, the stylus oscillates. The frequency of back-and-forth motion of the stylus is given by the speed of motion of the groove divided by the length of one wave on the disc. That is,

$$f = \frac{S_{\text{groove}}}{\lambda} \qquad\qquad (5.1)$$

The speed of the groove is different for different parts of the disc. The outer grooves move quite fast as compared to the inner grooves. For example, on a 30-cm diameter, long-play disc rotating at 33 ⅓ rev/min, the outer grooves (at a radius of 14 cm, say) would have a speed given by the circumference of the groove ($2\pi \times$ radius) times the number of revolutions per second (N_{rot}).

$$S = 2\pi r \, N_{\text{rot}} \qquad\qquad (5.2)$$

$$= 2 \times 3.14 \times 14 \text{ cm} \times \frac{33 \frac{1}{3} \text{ rev}}{60 \text{ s}} = 49 \frac{\text{cm}}{\text{s}}$$

However, the inner grooves have a much smaller radius and therefore a slower speed. For a radius of 6.5 cm the speed of the groove is

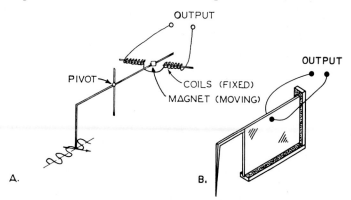

Fig. 5.3.   Schematic drawing for pickup devices. A: Magnetic. B: Piezoelectric.

$$S = 2\pi r\ N_{\text{rot}}$$

$$= 2 \times 3.14 \times 6.5\ \text{cm} \times \frac{33\ \tfrac{1}{3}\ \text{rev}}{60\ \text{s}} = 23\ \frac{\text{cm}}{\text{s}}$$

Suppose we wish to record a 1000-Hz signal. The resulting separations of deviations (λ in Fig. 5.2) on the disc will be different for the outer and the inner grooves. That is, from Eq. (5.1),

$$\lambda = \frac{S_{\text{groove}}}{f} = \frac{49\ \text{cm/s}}{1000\ \text{c/s}} = 0.049\ \text{cm}$$

while for the inner grooves,

$$\lambda = \frac{23\ \text{cm/s}}{1000\ \text{c/s}} = 0.023\ \text{cm}$$

The *same* audio signal will produce differently spaced groove deviations and different mechanical wavelengths on different parts of the disc.

5.1.2 Amplitude Information on Discs

The amplitude of the deviation of the groove (displacement) carries information about the amplitude of the original audio signal. To see how this amplitude information can be reproduced, recall that the output of a magnetic microphone depends on the speed of motion of the diaphragm. The same is true for a magnetic pickup device such as that shown in Fig. 5.3A. The voltage output is given by

$$V = Blv \tag{5.3}$$

where V is voltage, B is the strength of the magnet, l is the effective length of the coil, and v is the relative velocity between the coil and the magnet. (As the stylus moves, it carries with it the magnet, producing relative motion of the coil and magnet. Because the motions of stylus and magnet/coil are related, we consider v in the equation to be the velocity of the stylus.)

Consider two grooves on a disc, both containing deviations that produce 1000-Hz signals when played back. Suppose one groove has a *displacement* twice as great as the other; that is, the amplitude of the deviation of one groove is twice the amplitude of the second groove. The frequency is the same; thus as the stylus tracks the two grooves, it vibrates the same number of times per second for each groove. But for the first groove the stylus must move farther in the same amount of time because of the larger deviations. The result is that the speed of motion of the stylus, moving back and forth, is greater for the groove with the larger amplitude. Because the speed is greater, the output voltage from the pickup is greater. Thus, the amplitude of deviations in the groove carries the information of the amplitude of the audio signal.

To obtain some physical feeling for the size of the deviation of the groove, we call on a relationship, derived from the theory of simple harmonic motion, that the maximum velocity or speed of the stylus v_{max} is related to the frequency f and the amplitude A of the motion by the following:

$$v_{max} = 2\pi f A \tag{5.4}$$

Using this relation we may determine A if we know f and v. Present recordings, though not standardized, are normally adjusted so that the stylus velocity for the loudest sound on the disc is about 5 cm/s. (One may find recordings with five times that value.) Using 5 cm/s as typical, we may calculate the largest groove deviation:

$$A_{max} = \frac{v_{max}}{2\pi f} = \frac{5 \text{ cm/s}}{2 \times 3.14 \times 1000 \text{ c/s}} \cong 8 \times 10^{-4} \text{ cm} = 0.0008 \text{ cm}$$

Note that this very small distance is the maximum deviation. We can get some feeling for the minimum useful deviation by considering the dynamic range of modern commercial disc recordings. Although a dynamic range around 60 dB is possible on discs, around 50 dB is more common as a practical range. This 50-dB range corresponds to an intensity variation of $I_{max} = 10^5 I_{min} = 100,000 I_{min}$. Recall from Eq. (1.7) that intensity is proportional to the square of amplitude. We have then

$$\frac{I_{max}}{I_{min}} = \frac{(A_{max})^2}{(A_{min})^2} \tag{5.5}$$

$$\frac{A_{max}}{A_{min}} = \sqrt{\frac{I_{max}}{I_{min}}} = \sqrt{100,000} = 3.2 \times 10^2$$

The maximum allowed amplitude for a 1000-Hz signal is 320 times larger than the useful minimum amplitude. Therefore,

$$A_{min} = \frac{A_{max}}{320} = \frac{8 \times 10^{-4}\text{cm}}{320} = 2.5 \times 10^{-6} \text{ cm} = 0.0000025 \text{ cm}$$

(The size of a hydrogen atom is about 1×10^{-8} cm, so this deviation is about the size of 250 hydrogen atoms side by side!) Any signal with an amplitude smaller than this A_{min} would not be useful, since discrepancies in the groove shape, dirt in the groove, etc., may easily be this size. That is, a smaller signal would be lost in the "noise" created by disturbances in the groove.

The relation shown in Eq. (5.4) presents a problem. We have seen that for signals with frequencies of 1000 Hz, the typical maximum amplitude is about 8×10^{-4} cm. Note for 100-Hz signals, the maximum amplitude is 10 times larger since

$$A_{max} = \frac{v}{2\pi f} = \frac{5 \text{ cm/s}}{2 \times 3.14 \times 100 \text{ c/s}} = 8 \times 10^{-3} \text{ cm}$$

and the maximum amplitude for signals of 10,000 Hz is 10 times smaller:

$$A_{max} = \frac{v}{2\pi f} = \frac{5 \text{ cm/s}}{2 \times 3.14 \times 10,000 \text{ c/s}} = 8 \times 10^{-5} \text{ cm}$$

This means that low frequency signals cause (relatively) very large deviations of the groove, and high frequency signals have small amplitudes even for loud input sound. The large deviations for the bass signals require that the grooves be spaced far apart on the disc; thus, less recorded material per disc. The high frequency signals have small amplitudes; thus they are contaminated by noise signals from very small irregularities in the grooves.

The standard method for solution of these problems is called "equalization." With this technique, bass signals are reduced in amplitude when recorded and treble signals are increased. The present standard as accepted by the National Association of Broadcasters (NAB) and the Record Industry Association of America (RIAA) is shown in Fig. 5.4. Note that when the sound is reproduced from the disc, it is necessary to increase the bass and decrease the treble to account for adjustments made during recording. Such equalization is built into commercial playback equipment. The final output audio result is equivalent to the original audio signal.

5.1.3 Multichannel Storage on Discs

Up to now we have considered only one audio signal for the stored information. This approach, called monophonic for "one sound," has been replaced by multichannel recording techniques. The system most commonly in use at present is known as stereophonic reproduction, carrying two sets of discrete, independent information in one groove of the disc. (Quadraphonic systems are discussed in Chapter 8.) With our previous discussions of magnetic fields and how those fields interact with coils we can understand how two independent channels of information may be retrieved from one groove. Consider the pickup illustrated in Fig. 5.5, similar to the pickups in Fig. 5.3. Note here that motion of the stylus will cause two independent types of motion of the crossed plate: rotation about the vertical and about the horizontal axis. Furthermore, rotation about the horizontal axis will in no way influence the horizontal arm of the cross, and rotation about the vertical axis will not influence the vertical arm of the cross. Therefore, lateral motion of the stylus could be used to generate voltage in coils A and C, while vertical motion of the stylus could be used to generate voltage in B and D. Thus, we

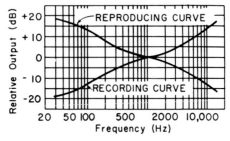

Fig. 5.4. Reproducing and recording characteristic curves as accepted by NAB and RIAA. (If both curves are used, final output signal response will be "flat.")

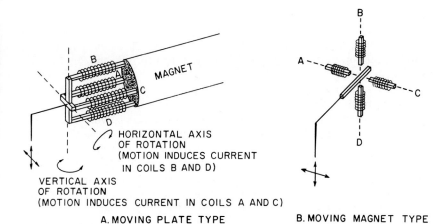

Fig. 5.5. Pickups in which horizontal motion of stylus induces electron flow in coils *A* and *C* and vertical motion induces flow in coils *B* and *D*.

may store two independent sets of information in one record groove by using lateral groove deviations for one and vertical groove deflections for the other.

The technique for storing two sets of information as vertical and horizontal deflections is not used in that form. The reason is simple. When stereo recordings were first produced, many of the playback systems in use were still monophonic, and the pickup units would respond only to lateral displacements of the groove. If a lateral-vertical stereo disc were reproduced on such a system, all the information in the vertical track would have been lost. Thus, to make the new stereo records playable (compatible) with the old monophonic systems, the stereo grooves were rotated to a 45°–45° tilt as shown in Fig. 5.6. Motion of either

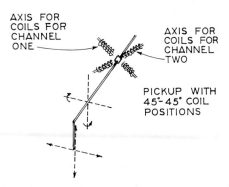

Fig. 5.6. Groove deviations and pickup design for 45°–45° two-channel disc systems.

channel will produce some lateral, thereby exciting even the old mono-phonic pickups. The two types of displacement are still at right angles to each other, however, so that in a stereo 45°–45° pickup system there is no interaction of the two independent sets of information. See Fig. 5.7 for illustration of a stereo cartridge.

These systems are not perfect. Even though the groove on the record may contain pure channel one information, when it is reproduced by a stylus some of that information may appear in channel two. This effect is called *cross talk*. The reason that cross talk occurs can be seen most easily perhaps from Fig 5.5A. In that drawing we see that even if the motion of the stylus is purely horizontal, the vertical plate rotates very slightly. This small motion of the vertical plate will produce a very small signal in the vertical channel. Thus, because of the finite size of the pickup elements and the fact that the lateral motion of the stylus is translated into rotational motion of the active magnetic element, cross talk is produced. In high quality stereo equipment this effect may be kept insignificantly small with the unwanted signal being at least 30 dB weaker than the primary signal.

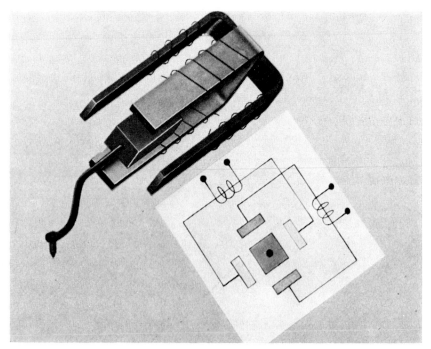

Fig. 5.7.   Drawing of stereo cartridge that employs moving magnet concept. (Drawing supplied by Shure Brothers, Inc., Evanston, Ill. Used by permission.)

5.2 MAGNETIC STORAGE AND RETRIEVAL FROM TAPE

In this section we discuss methods of storing audio signals with magnetic materials. As we have seen, it is simple to convert electrical signals into magnetic signals; we merely pass the electric current through a coiled conductor and the flow of electrons creates a magnetic field along the axis of the coil. Furthermore, we have seen that if we put a soft-iron core through the coil, the core will become magnetic when current flows in the coil. By bending the soft-iron material into some useful shape, we may direct the magnetic field into specific locations. The recording head of a tape recorder (Fig. 5.8) is designed according to these principles. The permeable material is bent into an almost closed loop with a very small gap between the pole pieces. The shape of pole pieces and gap are chosen so that a strong magnetic field exists in and near the gap whenever there is current in the coil.

5.2.1 Magnetism and Signal Storage

The recording head described above is useful for creating a magnetic field but alone it does not provide means for storing a signal. To understand how one may store a signal in magnetic materials, we need to consider the origin of magnetic fields. We have seen that a flow of electrons creates a magnetic field. The motion of any charge will create a magnetic field, and no magnetic field can be created without the motion of some charge. This last statement is interesting because it raises the question of how a piece of iron can have a magnetic field without being attached to any current source such as a battery. The answer lies in the structure of each single iron atom. We are all aware of drawings representing atoms as dense nuclei containing protons and neutrons surrounded by clouds of electrons. As it orbits the nucleus, each electron is an effective "electron current" that produces a magnetic field. This field is due to the orbital motion of the electron. In addition each electron is spinning. This also appears to be current since charge is in motion, and this spin produces another magnetic field. The net magnetic

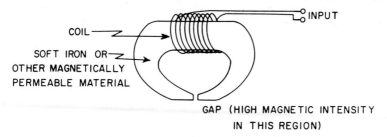

Fig. 5.8. Magnetic recording head. Separation in gap may be as large as 0.0025 cm (0.001 in) in professional recorders and as small as 0.0000025 cm in cassette recorders.

field for the atom is the sum of the contributions of all the electrons in the atom.

In most materials the sum of all electron contributions to magnetic field is zero since for every contribution with a north pole there is an equal and opposite contribution with a south pole. However in iron and other magnetic materials, the sum is not zero. Furthermore, some materials, not normally magnetic, become magnetic when alloyed with other materials.

The result is that iron is magnetic because each of its atoms is magnetic. This raises another question: how can a piece of iron not be magnetized, if each atom is magnetic? A piece of iron contains many atoms; a single iron filing could contain 10^{18} atoms. If these atoms were misoriented with respect to each other, the net result would be zero magnetic field for the whole body. For each north atom-magnet, there would be a south atom-magnet. In actual practice, the atoms do group together into "domains," regions in which all the atomic magnets are aligned. (A domain might contain about 10^{14} atoms.) In the bulk material these domains are misaligned with respect to each other such that the sum of the magnetic fields of all the domains is zero net magnetization. A magnetic piece of iron is one in which many domains are aligned in one direction (see Fig. 5.9).

We may use the technique of ordering magnetic domains to store a signal with magnetism. If one part of a body has magnetic domains ordered in one direction, the next part has domains ordered in the opposite direction, the next part ordered as the first, etc., we have in effect stored a signal. That signal may later be retrieved by passing the body near another head similar to the recording head. As the ordered domains in the body pass the head, the magnetic field of the domains will pass through the head and induce a voltage on the coil.

The original magnetic recordings were made on a long magnetic wire. It is common now to use magnetic tape produced by binding very finely ground magnetic materials onto a plastic tape as shown in Fig. 5.10. The plastic carrier provides a flexible support for the magnetic material, and the binder allows for freedom of orientation of the magnetic powder particles.

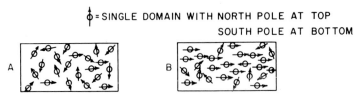

Fig. 5.9. A: Magnetic material with disordered domains; zero net magnetization. B: Magnetic material with some domains aligned; net magnetization of material.

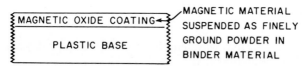

Fig. 5.10. Magnetic recording tape showing magnetic coating on plastic base.

Both the recording and playback processes are illustrated in Fig. 5.11. An alternating electrical signal is supplied to the coil of the recording head, producing an alternating magnetic field in the gap. As the tape passes by, those domains near the gap when a field is present become ordered and remain ordered after leaving the gap. As the ordered domains pass the playback head, they create a magnetic field in the head and thereby induce a voltage in the output coil.

5.2.2 Information Storage and Limits on Storage

Let us consider the stored information. As in the case of storage on discs, it is immediately apparent that at least two types of information may be stored, namely frequency and amplitude. Amplitude information is carried by the number of domains ordered in a particular region of the tape. That is, as the number of ordered domains increases, the strength of the magnetic field due to those domains increases and produces a larger output voltage when reproduced. Note that there is a maximum possible amplitude corresponding to the ordering of all domains in a given region.

Frequency is stored by spacing between ordered regions of the tape. As the tape passes by the reproducing head, the output voltage will vary with a frequency given by $f = $ (speed of tape)/(spacing between successive north domain poles), or

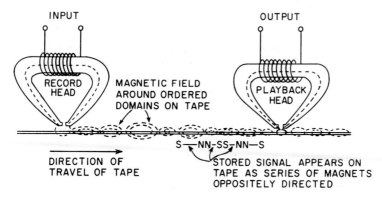

Fig. 5.11. Recording and playback processes schematically illustrated. Dotted lines represent lines of magnetic field. Recording and playback heads are identical in principle.

$$f = \frac{v_{\text{tape}}}{\lambda} \tag{5.6}$$

where λ is the effective wavelength of the audio signal as recorded on the tape. It is clear that if the speed of the playback system is different from the speed used during recording, the output frequency will be different from that initially recorded.

Two physical restrictions limit the upper frequency range for magnetic recording: (1) the size of the magnetic domains on the tape and (2) the size of the gaps in the reproducing and recording heads. The problem of domain size can be seen from the following. Suppose we wish to record a 10,000-Hz signal on tape moving at a speed of $1\frac{7}{8}$ in/s (the speed commonly used by cassette recorders). From Eq. (5.6) the wavelength on the tape will be

$$\lambda = \frac{v_{\text{tape}}}{f} = \frac{1.875 \text{ in/s}}{10,000 \text{ c/s}} = 1.875 \times 10^{-4} \text{ in } (= 4.8 \times 10^{-4} \text{ cm})$$

This is the spacing between successive north poles on the recorded signal on the tape. The smallest number of domains that could make up this signal is two, ordered as (N–S) (S–N). Thus,

$$\text{minimum domain size} = \frac{\lambda_{\text{min}}}{2} \tag{5.7}$$

For our example, the domain size must be at least as small as 2.4×10^{-4} cm for that signal to exist on the tape. In recent years special tape materials have been produced with domain size of the order of 2×10^{-5} cm, even smaller than required.

The size of the gap in the transducer heads also affects the upper frequency response. Suppose the gap is wide enough that a complete wavelength of the recorded signal can be spaced between the pole pieces, as shown in Fig. 5.12A. Note that essentially no magnetic field is created in the pole pieces since both pole pieces are near north poles, and there is no tendency of magnetic field lines to pass between similar magnetic poles. In Fig. 5.12B however, a maximum field is created in the pole pieces since one is near a north pole and the other near a south pole. The magnetic field lines pass through the pole piece magnet because that route is "easier" (the soft iron becomes magnetic) than passing through the air only. The result is that the size of the gap creates an effective upper frequency limit according to

$$d_{\text{gap}} = \frac{\lambda_{\text{min}}}{2} \tag{5.8}$$

The maximum frequency will then be

$$f_{\text{max}} = \frac{v_{\text{tape}}}{\lambda_{\text{min}}} = \frac{v_{\text{tape}}}{2d_{\text{gap}}} \tag{5.9}$$

Our present magnetic tape technology has reached such a state of development that both of the above limiting problems have been over-

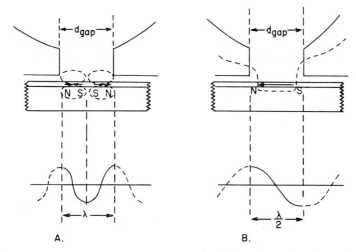

Fig. 5.12. A: Full wavelength of recorded signal between pole pieces. B: Half wavelength of recorded signal between pole pieces.

come for tape speeds as low as $1\frac{7}{8}$ in/s. Presently it is possible to record and to play back the full audible spectrum of frequencies on high quality $1\frac{7}{8}$-in/s machines. (These statements are not intended to imply that cassette machines are now equal in performance to reel-to-reel machines; this question is discussed in Section 5.2.5.)

5.2.3 Recording with Bias Frequency

Our discussion of recording on magnetic tape has been intentionally simplified. We now consider the processes involved in the response of an unmagnetized material to an external magnetic field. Suppose we put an unmagnetized piece of iron into a coil as in Fig. 5.13A. In B we show the typical response in the sample to an external field. Initially (a) no external field exists because no current is in the coil. Now we slowly increase the current until the external field has reached some value, H_{max}. The sample becomes magnetized as we follow the curve to b. Let us realize that when a piece of soft iron or other permeable material is placed in a magnetic field, the material develops its own magnetic field. The result is that B inside the material is much larger than H, the driving field. In Fig. 5.13B the units of the vertical B axis may be a thousand times larger than the horizontal H axis. Note that at b the sample has become saturated (all domains are aligned); applying a large external field greater than H_{max} will produce essentially no change in the magnetization of the sample. That saturation magnetic intensity is labeled B_s.

Next we begin to decrease the current, reducing the input field. Let us reduce the current to zero so that the external field H is zero. Note that the sample remains magnetized at c. The value of magnetic intensity

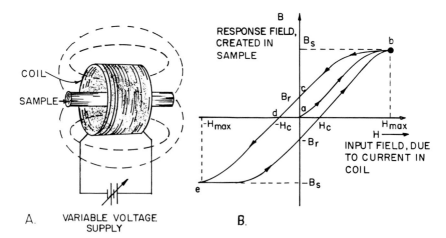

Fig. 5.13. A: Illustration of sample in external magnetic field due to current in a coil. B: Typical magnetic intensity response B to an input magnetic field H. Outer curves show magnetic hysteresis behavior.

remaining after the external field is removed is called the magnetic *retentivity*, B_r. Next we cause the current to flow in the opposite direction (bias signal), creating an oppositely directed input field. At d the field is strong enough to have removed all the remanent magnetism in the sample, which now has zero magnetization. This amount of input magnetic field necessary to bring the sample back to zero magnetization is called magnetic *coercivity*, H_c. Continuing to increase the reversal current we finally reach e where the sample has once again reached saturation.

Any further changes in the input field between $\pm H_{max}$ will cause the sample to follow the outer curves of the loop. This behavior is known as *hysteresis*. The amount of magnetization in the sample depends on the past history of the sample. The exact shape of the hysteresis curve and the values B_s, B_r, and H_c depend on the particular sample material.

This general discussion has application to our consideration of the process of recording on magnetic tape. Suppose that when a tape leaves the region close to the recording head gap, the field in the gap is H_1. How much magnetism is left on the tape? The retained value of magnetism is less than the magnetic retentivity B_r for the tape material as can be seen from Fig. 5.14. As the tape moves far away from the head, the value of the external field as sensed by the tape will drop to zero, even though an intense field H_1 may still be in the gap of the head itself. The sample demagnetizes, following a smaller hysteresis loop as drawn, and the amount of retained magnetization is B_1.

If we perform the above experiment for many different values of H_{input}, each time measuring the retained magnetization on the tape, we

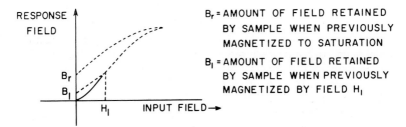

Fig. 5.14. Plot showing amount of magnetism retained in sample after different states of initial magnetization.

find a relation called the transduction curve as shown in Fig. 5.15. The important point to notice is that the curve is not linear; that is, it is not a straight line and will cause distortion in our recording if not corrected. For example, if we record two signals with input magnetizations H_2 and H_1 where H_2 is twice as great as H_1, we see from the curve that the retained magnetization B_2 is not twice B_1. Distortion has resulted, since the characteristics of the recorded signal do not agree with those of the input signal.

Note that the transduction curve does have some regions that are, for practical purposes, straight lines. The input signals H_2, H_3, and H_4 lie in the linear region. The change in the input signal from H_3 to H_4 is twice as great as the change from H_2 to H_3, and the change in the retained magnetization from B_3 to B_4 is twice as great as that from B_2 to B_3. Thus, the input signal has been stored with a linear response.

There is a technique to ensure that all recording is kept within the linear portions of the transduction curve. A very high frequency (of the order of 100,000 Hz), large amplitude signal is added to the input signal. This high frequency signal is called the bias frequency. Its effect is to

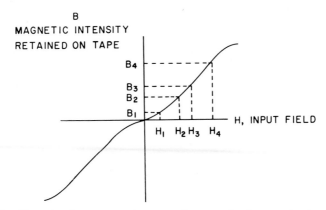

Fig. 5.15. Transduction curve. Amount of magnetization retained on tape as function of magnetic field at recording head.

produce an average state of input magnetic field in the center of the
linear region of the transduction curve. The small changes in the input
field due to the audio input merely cause small deviations around this
average magnetization produced by the bias frequency. These small deviations remain in the linear portion of the transduction curve, and the
recorded signal is not distorted (see Fig. 5.16).

We see from Fig. 5.16 that there is an optimum amplitude for the
bias frequency signal appropriate to a particular magnetic tape. Just as
the hysteresis curve depends on the particular material, so does the transduction curve. Thus, each recording tape has its own transduction curve
and its own value of the appropriate amplitude of the bias frequency.
A given tape recorder has certain amplitude bias frequency. (Newer
models have switches to allow the user to choose among different amplitudes to match different types of recording tape.) For best results one
should select a tape appropriate for the recorder.

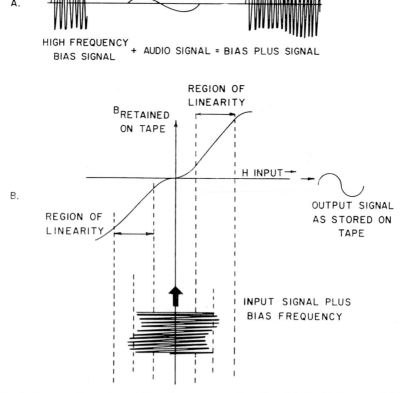

Fig. 5.16. A: Summing of bias frequency and audio signal. B: Input of bias
frequency and audio signal to transduction curve. If bias signal has proper
amplitude, resulting output signal will not be distorted.

5.2.4 Erasing

One of the most versatile characteristics of the magnetic tape medium is that a tape may be erased and rerecorded. Erasure is accomplished by the use of a transducer head similar to a recording head except in the size of the gap. The erase head commonly has a gap separation two hundred or so times larger than the recording head. A very high frequency signal of large amplitude is applied to the head (usually the same signal as that used for bias frequency). As the tape nears the region of the erase head gap, the domains on the tape are subjected to many complete reversals of orientation by the field in the gap. This continual reorienting destroys any previous orientation information of the domains. As the tape leaves the region near the gap, the field sensed by a given domain dies away to zero; the tape is left in a random state of orientation ready to be rerecorded.

Incidentally, it is possible to erase a magnetic tape accidentally. All that is needed is to give the magnetic particles on the tape enough energy to break their binder orientation and reorient themselves. This is surprisingly easy to do. For example, heating the tape (by laying it on a hot amplifier or near a heater vent) is sufficient to cause some reorientation. The presence of stray magnetic fields can cause reorientation. Even dropping the tape can free the particles for a split second, allowing them to be reoriented by either stray magnetic fields or the fields of the other parts of the same magnetic tape.

5.2.5 Limitations on Magnetic Tape Recording

Earlier we mentioned that recording systems using slow tape speeds can now reproduce the entire audio frequency range. Yet it should not be concluded that these machines are equivalent in performance to the machines that use faster tape transport speeds. Let us examine possible differences.

First, we compare frequency variation as a result of changes in tape transport speed. Suppose that a particular tape machine has a drive motor that transports the tape at 1.875 ± 0.005 in/s ($1\frac{7}{8}$ in/s speed). Then at any instant the actual tape speed may be any value in the range 1.870–1.880 in/s. The percentage error in the tape speed is then

$$\text{percentage error} = \frac{\Delta v}{v} \times 100\% = \frac{0.005 \text{ in/s}}{1.875 \text{ in/s}} \times 100\% = 0.27\%$$

Recall that the frequency f of the sound produced from the tape will be changed, since from Eq. (5.6), $f = v_{\text{tape}}/\lambda$. The absolute change in the frequency f due to an error in the speed v will be $\Delta f = \Delta v/\lambda$, and the fractional change will be

$$\frac{\Delta f}{f} = \frac{\Delta v/\lambda}{v/\lambda} = \frac{\Delta v}{v}$$

Thus, if the speed of the tape varies by 0.27%, then the frequency of the sound produced also varies by 0.27%. Although this error seems to be very small, let us note that for midrange frequencies (1000–5000 Hz), most people can hear a frequency change of 0.1%. ◄—— ✱ ✱ ✱

For comparison, suppose we operate the tape recorder at a speed of $7\frac{1}{2}$ in/s with the same absolute error (7.500 ± 0.005 in/s). Because the speed is much greater, the percentage error is now considerably smaller than before:

$$\text{percentage error} = \frac{\Delta v}{v} \times 100\% = \frac{0.005 \text{ in/s}}{7.500 \text{ in/s}} \times 100\% = 0.07\%$$

This result is less than the frequency discrimination range of most people (0.1%). Therefore, the same absolute speed error produces audible frequency variation at slow tape speeds but not at higher tape speeds. (Of course, it is possible to have speed drifting so great as to create audible frequency drift even at the fastest tape speeds.) No wonder commercial recording installations routinely use 15 in/s or 30 in/s as working tape speeds. The faster the speed, the smaller the percentage error for a given absolute error.

A second problem relating to tape speeds concerns the size of the gap in the transducer head. We have discussed how the size of the gap is determined by the maximum frequency response desired. From Eq. (5.9), we see that

$$d_{\text{gap}} = \frac{v_{\text{tape}}}{2f_{\text{max}}}$$

where f_{max} is our desired maximum frequency. Suppose we consider the two tape speeds, $1\frac{7}{8}$ in/s and $7\frac{1}{2}$ in/s. The faster speed is four times greater than the slow speed. Thus, the gap for $7\frac{1}{2}$-in/s tape work can be four times larger than for $1\frac{7}{8}$-in/s speeds.

We might ask if we would want to have the gap for $7\frac{1}{2}$-in/s recording to be four times greater than the gap for $1\frac{7}{8}$-in/s recording. After all, the technology exists for producing the narrow gap required for slow speeds; why not use it? The answer is that we need the largest possible gap. Recall that magnetic lines pass from one pole piece to the other. If the gap is very narrow, most of these lines are concentrated between the pole pieces and only a small percentage pass around the gap into the region occupied by the tape. Thus, as the recording gap is made narrower, the magnetic field in the tape weakens. On playback the efficiency of transfer of signal from tape to head is also reduced, again meaning weaker signals.

Furthermore, the amplitude of the signal recorded on or played back from a tape is very sensitive to "dropout," which occurs when the tape is pulled away from the head slightly because of a dust particle or nonuniform pressure from the device holding the tape against the head. If the gap is small, dropout causes a severe lowering of amplitude because the field lines do not extend uniformly away from the narrow gap region (see Fig. 5.17).

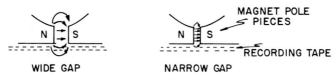

Fig. 5.17. Diagram of magnetic field lines between wide and narrow gaps (exaggerated).

Another significant difference between reel-to-reel machines and cassette machines is concerned with amplitude. We recall that the amplitude information on a tape is carried by the number of magnetically ordered domains. Cassette recorders use tape width $\frac{1}{8}$ in; other machines use $\frac{1}{4}$-in tape. Twice as much material means twice as many domains available for ordering, allowing a 3 dB greater dynamic range for the wider tape. Again, some commercial recording systems use tape wider than $\frac{1}{4}$ in to increase the available dynamic range.

5.2.6 Multichannel Information on Tape

The tape medium is simplest for storage of multichannel information. In Section 5.1.3 we discuss how to put two channels of independent information on discs. With present technology (discussed in Chapter 8) we are able to put four channels of information in one groove on a disc. At present that appears to be the reasonable upper limit. However, magnetic tape in principle is not limited to the number of independent channels available. Indeed, commercial recording machines are presently producing thirty-two tracks on a single magnetic tape.

We have discussed recording one signal on a tape, where the track of the signal encompasses the whole available width of the tape. To record a single signal but to double the available amount of time on the tape, we can record our signal on the top half of the tape only. Then, when we reach the end, we can turn over the tape and start recording again on this "new" top half. (This part is still blank when we turn the tape over because it was on the bottom half during the first recording.) The result is two tracks, recorded in opposite directions, as shown in Fig. 5.18.

Stereophonic (two-sound) information may be stored in two identical side-by-side tracks recorded in the same direction.

The most common reel-to-reel system is four track, also shown in Fig. 5.18. The four tracks are parallel with small separations. Tracks 1 and 3 carry the two stereo channels when the tape is traveling to the right as shown; and when the tape is inverted as described above, tracks 2 and 4 are used.

Note that these multitrack machines require special transducer heads. A possible head configuration for a four-track stereo system is shown in Fig. 5.19.

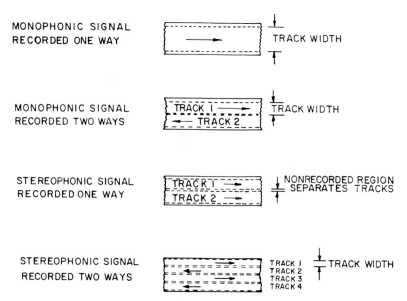

Fig. 5.18. Formats for various recording schemes. Note decreasing track width with increasing sophistication of information storage.

We must realize that with all the advantages that come from putting multichannel information on one tape (such as longer playing time, stereo effect, etc.), something is lost. By using a narrower channel we have less magnetic material in the region of the (now smaller) gap of the transducer head, which means that the available dynamic range is reduced and the available signals are weaker. Amplitude and dynamic range are reduced when channel size is reduced. Also, consider the obvious mechanical details of alignment—a small change in alignment can have a large effect if the narrow track is displaced away from the gap in the transducer head.

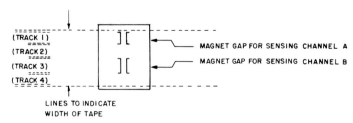

Fig. 5.19. Transducer head for stereo four-track system. Two magnetic gaps are indicated: each is separate magnet-coil system. The two gaps are positioned to sense tracks 1 and 3 for one tape configuration. If tape is turned over (or if head is shifted down), same gaps sense tracks 2 and 4.

5.2.7   Tape Noise and Dolby Reduction System

It is well known that even unrecorded tape will produce a hiss when played back. We can understand why this happens if we consider the arrangement of the domains on the tape. If no signal is on the tape (unrecorded or erased), we would expect a totally random distribution of domains such that the average magnetization at any point is zero. On a very large scale this might be true, but in a small region the size of the gap, it is likely that even a random distribution will sometimes have more domains ordered in one direction than another. In fact, according to the discipline in physics called statistical mechanics, fluctuations in the random distribution of the domains are to be expected. These fluctuations, although not repeating in a wavelike pattern along the tape like music signals, do produce magnetization in the playback head. Thus, we hear a hiss corresponding to pulses of sound with no uniform repetition rate.

Again, we have a potential problem with small track size. The relative strength of these fluctuations (that is, the number of ordered domains as compared to the total number of domains in a given region) grows as the width of channel size is reduced and as the separation of the gap is decreased. In fact, statistical mechanics helps us predict the relative effect: the number of ordered domains in a fluctuation is a quantity that depends on the square root of the number of available domains. Let us compare the relative strength of the fluctuations for two cases where the number of domains is, say, 1000 and 10,000. For the 1000-domain case,

$$\text{relative strength } \alpha \ \sqrt{1000}/1000 \ = \ 33/1000 \ = \ 0.033$$

For the 10,000-domain case,

$$\text{relative strength } \alpha \ \sqrt{10,000}/10,000 \ = \ 100/10,000 \ = \ 0.01$$

We see that for the 1000-domain case the strength of the fluctuation is three times larger than for the 10,000-domain case. The smaller the number of domains (small tracks, small gaps), the larger the hiss caused.

Note that the hiss is most objectionable for quiet portions of recorded tapes. The hiss is always there, even for recorded material. However, the level of the hiss signal is low and is only noticeable when the recorded signal is of low amplitude also. [The Dolby noise reduction system is specifically designed to reduce hiss (and other noise) during quiet passages.]✳ ✳ ✳

The Dolby system is a two-step procedure: (1) the original recording is altered in a well-defined manner and (2) on playback the alterations are compensated and corrected. Let us consider the two steps. Suppose we sketch the recorded amplitude versus the input amplitude, as shown in Fig. 5.20. Note that in the Dolby system, weak input signals are boosted when recorded. In practice, since it is the high frequency components that normally have low amplitudes, the system boosts mainly the high frequency components. When the tape is played back, some-

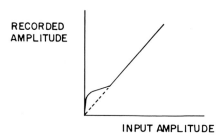

Fig. 5.20. Recorded amplitude versus input amplitude for linear (dotted line) and Dolby (solid line) recording techniques.

thing must be done to compensate for the boosting or the low, quiet passages will reproduce much louder than they were originally.

Note that the overall curve is sloped. This is the "recording characteristic" for tape recording and is similar to the recording characteristic for disc recording discussed in Section 5.1.2. This technique is used to ensure that, on the tape, signals of all frequencies have reasonable amplitudes, neither so large that they saturate the tape nor so small that they are weaker than the random tape magnetizations that produce noise and hiss.

When the signal is played back, the signal must be transformed back to the original linear characteristics. Figure 5.21 shows a representation of this process. The solid line represents the signal as recorded with the high frequency signals boosted in amplitude. A filter circuit selects out the high frequency components and reduces their amplitudes, bringing the overall reproduced signal back to a linear relation of amplitude and frequency. The significant gain from this technique is that the hiss is also reduced in the high frequency range where hiss is most objectionable. If Dolby-recorded material is played on non-Dolby playback equipment, high frequency components will appear quite strong.

5.3 RECORDING SOUND SIGNALS ON FILM

5.3.1 Magnetic Sound Track

One system used for home recording is shown in Fig. 5.22. The sound track is simply a strip of magnetic recording tape that is recorded

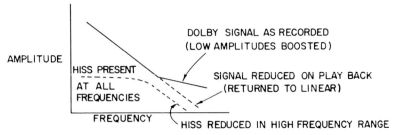

Fig. 5.21. Typical Dolby playback corrections.

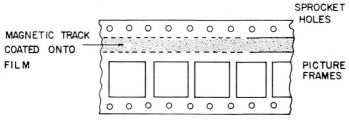

Fig. 5.22.   Magnetic sound track on film.

and bonded to the film at the time of the development process. A magnetic transducer head is used to sense the recorded signal.

This method is not used for commercial theaters because constant use causes deterioration of the magnetic head. This problem is not encountered in home movie situations since the total amount of use of such systems is actually quite small.

5.3.2   Optical Sound Track

Another means of sensing a signal is with a varying-intensity light. This method involves the use of photocells or tubes that emit electric current when struck with light and do not emit current when the light is removed. The design of the tubes is similar to the simple diode vacuum tubes discussed in Section 3.2. But in the photocell there is no hot filament (see Fig. 5.23). The release of the electrons occurs because of a particular characteristic of light (and of all waves).

Light behaves in some experiments as if it were a wave. We shall discuss the wave nature of light in Chapter 6 when we deal with radio. However, in some other experiments light behaves as if it were composed of *particles*. These particles have been given the name *photons,* and their properties are well understood. For example, the energy of one photon is related to the frequency of the light. The relation, given by Albert Einstein, is

$$E = hf \tag{5.10}$$

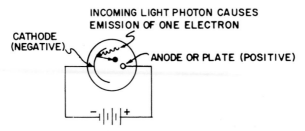

Fig. 5.23.   Diagram of simple photocell. Incoming photon of light strikes negative cathode and is absorbed by single electron; that electron then has enough energy to escape the metal and is attracted by positive anode.

where E is the energy of the photon, h is a number known as Planck's constant (6.6×10^{-34} J·s), and f is the frequency of the light. We find in Chapter 7 that the frequency of visible light is about 10^{15} Hz. Thus, the energy of a photon of visible light is typically about

$$E = (6.6 \times 10^{-34} \text{ J·s}) \times (10^{15} \text{ c/s}) \cong 7 \times 10^{-19} \text{ J}$$

A single photon appears to have a very small amount of energy. However, if a single electron in the (negative) cathode of the photocell absorbs a single photon, the electron may receive enough energy to escape from the metal. In fact, this is the experiment that first convinced people of the photon character of light. In a particular photocell device, red light (low frequency) would not cause electrons to leave the metal, no matter how bright the light was. Blue light (higher frequency), even when dim, caused electrons to leave the metal and flow through the tube. Einstein was right; light behaves as particles (photons) and the energy of the photons depends on the frequency. Red light photons do not have enough energy to free the electrons; blue light photons do.

In audiovisual optical track recording, we use this phenomenal behavior of photons and electrons to cause a varying current to flow in some audio circuit. The arrangement is shown in Fig. 5.24.

The optical track may be laid several ways. One method employs repeated dark-clear-dark-clear lines with the spacing giving the signal frequency and the thickness of the lines giving the amplitude information. Another technique uses a variable-density (clear/gray/black) track; the density fluctuations give the frequency and the blackness of the track gives the amplitude. In this system, uniformity in the film developing

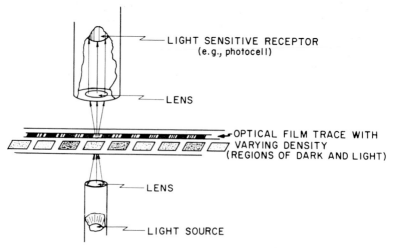

Fig. 5.24. Photoelectric detection system for variable-light-intensity sound track recording.

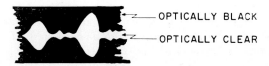

Fig. 5.25. Variable-area optical track.

process is critical. A third technique, perhaps the most common, employs a variable-area track as shown in Fig. 5.25. The repetition rate of the area fluctuations carries the frequency information, and the width of the clear area carries the amplitude information. This method has the advantage of using optically clear and optically black images on the film —thus the images are not nearly so sensitive to development uniformity.

5.4 DIGITAL STORAGE

The methods of storing audio signals that we have discussed are familiar to most people. In this section we examine a newer form of signal storage yet to become available on the consumer market: digital storage. This method holds promise of being essentially noise-free; that is, there is no surface noise as in grooved disc recording, no tape hiss as in conventional magnetic tape recording, and no nonlinear distortion as often found in optical film track recording and in both records and magnetic tapes.

Each of the conventional techniques is susceptible to noise because the desired signal and the noise both cause the same type of response in the detector. For example, as a stylus tracks the groove of a disc, the stylus moves in response to the oscillation of the groove. However, a dust particle on the surface of the record also causes the stylus to move. Thus, both noise and the signal excite the stylus in the same manner.

In a digital system, the response of the detector to the signal may be uniquely isolated from the response to noise; thus noise may be separated out and almost entirely eliminated.

Digital storage means two things: (1) representing the signal by a series of numbers and (2) storing those numbers. For example, if we wish to represent a sine wave digitally, we write down a list of numbers that represent the amplitudes of the wave for successive steps in time. If we choose large time slots, we will get a very choppy picture of the wave. If we choose narrow time slots, then we can recreate the original wave with a high degree of accuracy. A crude analogy can be made with the temperature chart of a patient in a hospital. Some medical personnel prefer to see a graph (waveform) of temperature variation; other staff people prefer to see a list (digital values) of the actual temperature values for each time period. Both the graph and the list contain the information, and either may be used to generate the other.

In a similar manner digital representations of signals are made. The voltage signal is fed into a device called an analog-to-digital converter, which essentially reads the voltage at each predefined time step (there can easily be a million time steps per second), and records on some device the value of the voltage (amplitude) at each step. To recreate the signal later, some other device simply reads the recorded numbers and generates voltages called for at each time step.

To store the set of values is actually as easy, if not easier, than to record the complete waveform itself by our conventional techniques. To see how it can be done, let us examine how we normally represent a number. Suppose we have 23 pencils. What does 23 mean? The symbol 23 means a set of objects containing

$$(2 \times 10^1) + (3 \times 10^0) \quad \text{or} \quad 20 + 3 = 23 \text{ objects}$$

Our normal counting method is in the base-10 or decimal system: we have 10 digits (0 through 9); then we start over. The number 1536 means

$$
\begin{aligned}
(1 \times 10)^3 &+ (5 \times 10^2) + (3 \times 10^1) + (6 \times 10^0) \\
= (1 \times 1000) &+ (5 \times 100) + (3 \times 10) + (6 \times 1) \\
= 1000 &\quad\;\; + 500 \quad\;\;\; + 30 \quad\;\; + 6 \\
= 1536
\end{aligned}
$$

When we think about it, we see that our normal method of counting is rather complicated.

A much simpler number system than the base-10 system is the base-2 or *binary* system. It is simpler because it has only two digits, 0 and 1. For example, in the binary system the symbol 101 represents the same thing that the symbol 5 represents in our base-10 system. We can see that by counting just as we did in the base-10 system. Binary 101 means adding together powers of 2 with

$$
\begin{aligned}
101 &= (1 \times 2^2) + (0 \times 2^1) + (1 \times 2^0) \\
&= 4 \quad\;\;\; + 0 \quad\;\;\; + 1 \\
&= 5
\end{aligned}
$$

Or, binary 10111 represents 23 since

$$
\begin{aligned}
10111 &= (1 \times 2^4) + (0 \times 2^3) + (1 \times 2^2) + (1 \times 2^1) \\
&\quad + (1 \times 2^0) \\
&= 16 \quad\;\; + 0 \quad\;\;\; + 4 \quad\;\;\; + 2 \quad\;\;\; + 1 \\
&= 23
\end{aligned}
$$

Our point here is not to learn binary counting (interesting though it may be), but rather to see that numbers, *all* numbers, may be written in a binary form made up only of 1s and 0s. The reason this is so very important is that 1s and 0s can be represented electronically by ON and OFF. If we have a string of five electronic switches, we can represent the number 23 by its binary form 10111 as

ON-OFF-ON-ON-ON

Furthermore, if those five switches controlled five battery circuits so that the one on the right produced 1 V (2^0), the next 2 V (2^1), the next 4 V

(2^2), etc., and we added the output together, we could create a 23-V output signal by

ON-OFF-ON-ON-ON

$$16 \text{ V} + 0 + 4 \text{ V} + 2 \text{ V} + 1 \text{ V} = 23 \text{ V}$$

In fact, we could make any integer voltage from 0 to 31 V by the appropriate setting of the five switches. (We could not make $9\frac{1}{2}$ V; our system has 1-V steps only. We must have smaller voltage steps to get greater resolution.)

The process of digital recording uses many binary digits to represent the voltage of the audio signal at each time step. These binary digits are then recorded as 1s or 0s on some medium such as photographic film, magnetic tape, or the newer magnetic "floppy" discs (flexible discs coated with magnetic material). The photographic film method employs a train of very small regions of light and dark. An optical scanning device then senses the image on the film and interprets it as a succession of 1s and 0s (binary numbers). A magnetic device can have a binary signal stored in either of two ways: (1) disordered magnetic domains (random) to represent 0 and ordered to represent 1 or (2) ordered one direction for 0 and the other direction for 1. Both the photograph and magnetic storage methods are amenable to mass production. The magnetic system also allows erasure and rerecording.

When the signal is reclaimed from these storage devices, the signal is, of course, composed of 0 and 1 states. This is the key to noise suppression. It is likely that any noise or hiss, etc., will be at some level different from either the 0 level or the 1 level of the detector. The detector may pick up noise, but it is simple electronically to screen the noise signals away; one constructs an electronic "gate" or filter that passes only voltages appropriate for the 0 and 1 states from the detector and blocks all other voltage signals. Such a gate is called a voltage discriminator and is rather easy to design.

In conclusion we mention that although the above techniques are not yet available on the consumer market, they are already being used in a great variety of communications applications and are well developed by the digital computer industry. We may predict that the consumer market will see the advent of these devices as soon as the costs of the detection systems can be made competitive with conventional equipment. In fact, the author has heard it stated in a scientific conference that "in the next ten years" grooved discs will disappear from the market to be replaced by digital devices. It will be interesting to see the outcome of this bold prediction.

5.5 SUMMARY

(1) Audio signals may be stored on discs with deviations of a mechanical groove cut into the material. The length from peak to peak of the deviations carries the frequency information, and the amplitude of the deviations carries the acoustic amplitude information.

(2) By cutting the groove with two independent motions 90° apart, two independent channels of information may be stored.

(3) The information from a groove in a disc may be reclaimed by tracking the groove with a stylus to which a magnet is attached. The motion of the magnet induces a changing voltage in nearby sensing coils. Two-channel information may be detected by the same single stylus-magnet combination with two sets of sensing coils whose axes are 90° apart.

(4) The ordering of magnetic material may be used to store information. The length from a north pole to the next north pole carries the frequency information, and the amount of ordered magnetic material carries the amplitude information.

(5) The macroscopic phenomenon of magnetism in a material is the result of a microscopic phenomenon—the constituent atoms of the material possess magnetic fields and those fields are aligned with one another. An atom is magnetic because the electrons of the atom are in motion. Electrons have two motions that produce magnetism: orbital motion (they orbit the nucleus) and a type of spin motion similar to the earth spinning on its axis. (Because advanced physical treatments show that the electron is not a solid ball, it is incorrect for us to say that it spins in the literal sense.) The net magnetic behavior of an atom is due to the sum of the magnetic fields of all the electrons in the atom.

(6) Magnetic recording tape is comprised of a finely ground magnetic material suspended in a binder material that adheres to a flexible plastic base. The size of the magnetic particles can limit the high frequency storage capability of the tape.

(7) Information may be transferred to the tape by a magnetic transducer head. The size of the gap in the head can limit the high frequency storage capability. The gap must be smaller than $\lambda_{min}/2$ where λ_{min} is the shortest wavelength (highest frequency) to be recorded.

(8) Magnetic materials exhibit hysteresis when subjected to an external magnetic field. That is, the amount of magnetization of the sample depends on the past history of the material.

(9) The hysteresis effect is responsible for the nonlinearity of a *transduction curve*. The amount of magnetization left in a tape is not linearly related to the input magnetic field. To alleviate this problem, a high frequency bias signal is added to the input signal when recording on magnetic tape. The bias signal produces an average magnetization that falls into a linear portion of the transduction curve.

(10) Magnetic tape may be erased by any process that causes or allows reorientation of the magnetic particles. Most tape recorders apply a high frequency signal to a transducer that causes a strong varying magnetic field to penetrate the tape. Heat or severe jarring will contribute to accidental erasure.

(11) Multichannel information is conveniently stored in independent tracks on a magnetic tape. However, the more channels on a single tape, the narrower the tracks. Any reduction in track width also re-

duces the available dynamic range for information to be stored.

(12) Noise reduction systems aid in removing tape "hiss," which arises from incomplete disorder of the domains along the tape. The Dolby system is a technique that boosts low amplitude signals on recording and then reduces the same signals on playback. Because the hiss is low amplitude, it is also reduced.

(13) Signals may be recorded on film by light and dark variations of a sound track. These variations are sensed by a device known as a photocell. The operation of the photocell is based on electrons absorbing single particles of light called photons.

(14) Digital storage methods can be used to eliminate noise in the signal storage process. The signal is represented by numbers that record the amplitude of the waveform at successive time steps. Binary numbers are usually employed, since they can be represented by ON-OFF states of electronic devices.

QUESTIONS

1. When audio signals are recorded by means of a grooved track on a disc, what carries the frequency information and what carries the amplitude (loudness) information?
2. Why is the recorded length of one wavelength of a 1000-Hz signal longer on the outer grooves of a disc than on the inner grooves?
3. Why are the amplitudes of bass frequency signals reduced when a recording is made?
4. How can two independent channels of information be recorded in one record groove?
5. Why is it important to keep a record clean?
6. When audio signals are recorded by means of a magnetic tape, how are the frequency and amplitude information stored?
7. Describe the advantages of using fast tape speeds and wide tracks on tape.
8. Why is "tape biasing" used?
9. What factors limit the frequency response of a tape recording signal?
10. How can a magnetic tape be erased?
11. What is the photoelectric effect?
12. How can an audio signal be recorded onto an optical track on a film? What are the factors limiting the frequency response and dynamic range of the recorded signal?
13. What is the meaning of "digital recording"?
14. Explain how frequency and amplitude information can be contained in digital records.
15. What are the advantages of digital recording over conventional techniques?

EXERCISES

1. Calculate the following for a 33⅓-rpm record:
   (a) speed of travel of the groove when the radius is 10 cm

(b) wavelength on the record for a frequency of 10,000 Hz at a radius of 10 cm

(c) highest frequency that may be reproduced by a stylus of spherical tip diameter 0.0025 cm (0.001 in) at a record radius of 10 cm. (The wavelength on the record must be at least twice as big as the tip.)

2. Suppose the width of a groove on a disc is 0.0004 cm. How many times that width will the amplitude of the groove deviation be for a 1000-Hz signal recorded to produce a stylus velocity of 5 cm/s? (Answer: 2)

3. Suppose that the groove on a disc has the appropriate amplitude deviation to cause a stylus to oscillate with a maximum speed of 5 cm/s. When that happens a voltage of 20 mV (millivolts; 1 mV = 10^{-3} V) is generated in the cartridge. What would the output voltage be if the amplitude were changed to give a maximum speed of 2 cm/s?

4. In a later chapter we discuss quadraphonic recording. One method of four-channel recording employs frequencies up to 45,000 Hz to be cut into a record groove. How small must a stylus tip be to track a groove at radius 6.5 cm being played at $33\frac{1}{3}$ rpm when the groove contains a 45-kHz signal? (The tip can be no larger than half a wavelength on the record track.)

5. What is the recorded wavelength of a 15,000-Hz signal on a magnetic tape moving at $17\frac{7}{8}$ in/s?

6. A cassette tape recorder has a head gap of 2.4×10^{-4} cm. What is the upper frequency limit of this machine? (Note: $17\frac{7}{8}$ in/s = 4.76 cm/s) (Answer: 9.9 kHz)

7. A tone of 1000 Hz is recorded by a high quality cassette recorder running at almost exactly 1.875 in/s. The tape is played back later on a machine running slowly at 1.800 in/s. What tone is reproduced? (Answer: 960 Hz)

8. A tone of 1000 Hz is recorded by a high quality reel-to-reel tape recorder running at almost exactly 7.500 in/s. The tape is played back later on a machine running slowly at 7.425 in/s (same absolute error as in Exercise 7). What tone is reproduced?

9. In our decimal (base-10) number system, the symbol 111 means $100 + 10 + 1$, and the symbol 234 means $(2 \times 100) + (3 \times 10) + (4 \times 1)$. What does the base-10 symbol 527.2 mean?

10. Convert the binary symbol 1101 into decimal notation. Express 17 in binary form. (Answers: 13; 10001)

11. Red and blue light waves have different frequencies. Compare the energy of photons of red light ($f = 4.3 \times 10^{14}$ Hz) with the energy of photons of blue light ($f = 7.5 \times 10^{14}$ Hz). Which color light would be more likely to cause electrons to be emitted from a metal surface?

6
PLAYBACK: LOUDSPEAKERS

We have dealt with the conversion of an audio signal into an electrical signal and operation on that electrical signal such as amplification or storage. If we wish to play back that signal, we must find some transducer that will convert an electrical signal into an acoustical form. Once again we are dealing with energy conversion; with electrical energy we wish to cause the motion (mechanical energy) of air molecules, thereby creating acoustical energy.

How much air do we actually need to move? An excellent discussion of this is presented by Olson, and his results are shown in Fig. 6.1. From the graph we see that to produce 1 W of acoustical output at 50 Hz we must cause the motion of 10^3 cm^3 (1 L) of air molecules, 50,000 times greater than that necessary to get 1 W output at 10^4 Hz. Immediately we may conclude that transducers for low frequency reproduction will be considerably larger than transducers appropriate for high frequency reproduction. Also we may conclude that if a single transducer is used to reproduce all audio frequencies, then the motion (or displacement) of the driving element will be large for low frequencies and small for high frequencies.

6.1 LOUDSPEAKERS

A *loudspeaker* is a transducer that can convert electrical signals to acoustical signals. There are many types of loudspeakers, many sizes, and even many shapes. We may note that we already know a considerable amount about the principles describing loudspeakers from our study of microphones. Recall that microphones are transducers that operate as acoustical to electrical converters. Loudspeakers are in principle microphones run "backwards." (This is not a far-fetched statement; many modern intercom systems use a single transducer to serve the functions of both microphone and loudspeaker.) The actual constructed design of microphones and loudspeakers may be very different, but the physical principles are the same for both.

In Fig. 6.2 we show a schematic representation of a magnetic (or dynamic) loudspeaker. The alternating electrical signal is applied to the voice coil. As current flows through the coil, a magnetic field is set

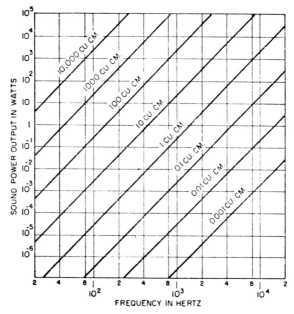

Fig. 6.1. Sound power output versus frequency for several quantities of air displaced per cycle. (From Harry F. Olson, *Modern Sound Reproduction*, p. 11; © 1971, Litton Educ. Publ., Inc. Reprinted by permission of Van Nostrand Reinhold Co.)

up along the axis of the coil. This field interacts with the field caused by the permanent magnet, and the coil is either pulled inward or pushed outward. The signal is always changing, so that the current in the coil is changing. Thus, the repulsion or attraction of the coil is changing. The result is that the coil moves inward or outward with the frequency of the incoming signal. Large amplitude signals cause large currents in the coil, causing large displacements of the coil. Because the coil is connected to the diaphragm, any motion of the coil also moves the cone and creates a pressure wave in the air around the loudspeaker.

Electrostatic loudspeakers are based on the same principle as the condenser microphones we discussed in Section 2.7. Two conducting plates are separated by an insulating material, and at least one plate is suspended so that it is movable (see Fig. 6.3.). A constant high voltage is supplied to the two plates so that one becomes highly positively charged and the other negatively charged. The movable plate is then attracted toward the fixed plate, and the system comes to an equilibrium configuration. If we also apply an input signal to the plates, the movable plate will move in and out slightly. When the input signal is of the same polarity as the high voltage source, the charges on the plate will increase slightly and the movable plate will be pulled inward slightly. When the input

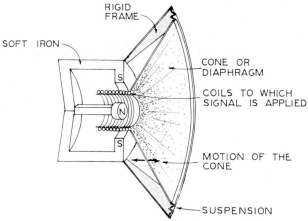

Fig. 6.2. Cutaway view of dynamic (or magnetic) loudspeaker. Note similarity to dynamic microphone in Fig. 2.4.

signal is of opposite polarity, the charges will decrease slightly, relaxing the attraction, and the suspension will pull the movable plate outward. The frequency of motion of the plate will be the same as the input signal, and the amplitude of the displacement will be directly proportional to the amplitude of the input signal.

What would happen if the signal *only* were applied to an electrostatic loudspeaker (the high voltage supply is removed)? When the input voltage is zero, the plates are uncharged and the movable plate sits at its equilibrium position. Now we apply a signal. Recall that the signal is composed of positive and negative peaks of voltage. Suppose that the first half of each oscillation makes the movable plate positive

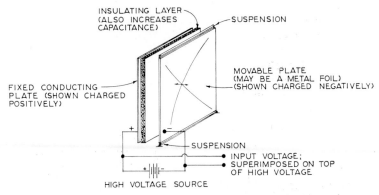

Fig. 6.3. Schematic illustration of electrostatic loudspeaker with one movable plate which may be made of thin metal or an aluminum coating on film of plastic.

and the fixed plate negative. The movable plate is pulled inward by the electrostatic attraction. The signal voltage returns to zero after the positive peak has passed, and the plate returns to its equilibrium position (with outward motion). Now the second half of the electrical oscillation is applied to the plates. The movable plate is made negative and the fixed plate positive, and the movable plate is pulled inward again. Even though the polarity on the plates has been changed, the force on the plate is again attraction. As the signal voltage returns to zero, the plate moves outward to the equilibrium position.

The signal has made *one* complete oscillation: zero, positive, zero, negative, zero. The plate has made *two* complete oscillations: inward, outward, inward, outward. If the input electrical signal had had frequency f_0, the output acoustical signal would have had frequency $2f_0$, one octave higher.

By applying the constant high voltage, we eliminate this frequency doubling. If the high voltage is V_0 and the signal voltage is $\pm V$ (much smaller than V_0), then the total voltage on the plates of the speaker will be $V_0 \pm V$, which will never reverse polarity. In practice V_0 may be as large as 2000 V, and V is typically ± 50 V. The voltage on the plates then varies between 2050 and 1950 V, always of the same polarity.

While discussing microphones we learned that a piezoelectric crystal will generate a voltage between its faces when the crystal is bent or distorted. Following this principle we may design a loudspeaker based on the bending of the piezoelectric crystal after a voltage is applied (see Fig. 6.4). The input voltage is applied across the faces of the crystal, which distorts in response to the electric field. This distortion is mechanically coupled to a diaphragm; as the crystal distorts, the cone moves and creates acoustical pressure waves.

It is quite difficult to produce the large, uniform piezoelectric crystals necessary to move the large volumes of air needed for reasonable sound power at low frequencies. Consequently, these crystal loudspeakers are employed most often in applications involving small physical size such as hearing aids or very small radios.

6.2. HORN COUPLING

Although a loudspeaker is simple in principle, there are problems in the use of such a transducer. The first problem we discuss concerns

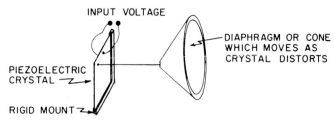

Fig. 6.4.   Illustration of crystal (or piezoelectric) loudspeaker.

the efficiency of conversion of electrical energy to acoustical energy. To
be efficient the loudspeaker must "couple" well to the air. The air acts
as a mechanical resistance to the loudspeaker. The input signal actually
drives not only the cone but also the body of air near the cone. For
example, if the input signal is of very high frequency, the cone must respond with a very rapid back-and-forth oscillation, each time moving
air. Suppose the cone were large, say, one foot in diameter. Then a
great amount of air would also have to move back and forth with high
frequency; the resistance of the air may be great enough to prevent the
cone from moving enough to be effective. The result is that the resistance to motion of the air may prevent the transducer from converting the electrical energy to acoustical energy.

One method of improving the mechanical coupling between the
loudspeaker and the air is with a horn. In a simplistic view, we might
think of the horn as matching the small area of the loudspeaker to the
large area where the sound is to be produced by the gradual increase of
diameter of the horn. The basic design of a horn has many variations;
we shall discuss the basic exponential horn.

In Fig. 6.5 we see the shape of the basic exponential horn. The
word exponential is used because the relation of the cross-sectional area
A_x to the area A_0 at the diaphragm depends on a power (exponent) involving x, the distance from the diaphragm. The relation is

$$A_x = A_0 \ e^{ax} \tag{6.1}$$

where: x = distance along axis of horn from diaphragm
A_x = cross-sectional area at distance x
A_0 = cross-sectional area of diaphragm
e = 2.718 . . . , the so-called natural number
a = $4\pi f_c / v_{sound}$
f_c = cutoff frequency for this horn (see below)

The cutoff frequency is the lowest frequency that can be efficiently
matched to the environment by the horn. For example, very low fre-

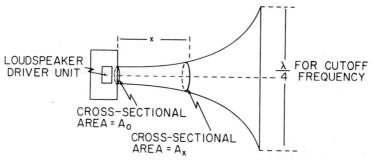

Fig. 6.5. Structural shape of basic exponential horn.

quencies have long wavelengths; the size of the horn opening may be much smaller than these long wavelengths. The result is that when these wavelengths are produced, they are so large that the horn opening is still too small to match effectively the diaphragm and the environment. The equation is not the important point in this discussion; that some waves will be efficiently matched and others not is the important point.

6.3 BAFFLES AND ENCLOSURES

Let us return to the problems associated with a single loudspeaker. Suppose we have a loudspeaker in open air as in Fig. 6.6. During outward motion of the cone, air in front of the cone is compressed to a pressure higher than atmospheric pressure, and the air behind the cone is decreased in pressure—a pressure or acoustic wave is created. However, the air from the high pressure side can flow around the edges of the speaker to the low pressure side, which is exactly what happens for low frequency, long wavelength acoustic waves. The result is that if the wavelength of a sound is larger than the dimensions of the speaker, the high pressure region will flow to cancel the low pressure region; and the intensities of the signals are severely reduced. At high frequencies the wavelengths are short, and the air does not have time to travel from front to back before a new wave is created in the rear. Thus there is little cancellation of high frequency waves.

A solution to this problem is to mount the loudspeaker in a "baffle" —a rigid mount whose dimensions are such as to prevent the air from the high pressure region from reaching the low pressure region before the wave has traveled away from the speaker (see Fig. 6.7). The path length D must be considerably greater than the wavelength of the low frequency signals. If D is large enough to prevent an appreciable flow of air from front to back for very low frequencies, the baffle is called an "infinite" baffle.

Using a baffle to prevent the pressure in front of a speaker from

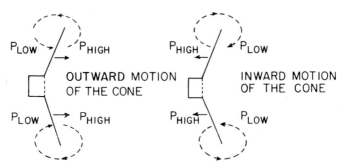

Fig. 6.6. Illustration of cancellation of pressure wave created by loudspeaker due to flow of air from high pressure to low pressure side.

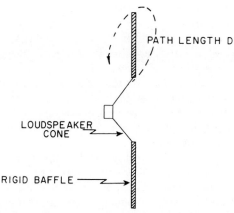

PATH LENGTH D

LOUDSPEAKER
CONE

RIGID BAFFLE

Fig. 6.7. Loudspeaker mounted in baffle.

cancelling some rear pressure leads one to suggest that putting the speaker into a box enclosure would eliminate all pressure cancellation! However, new problems are introduced by mounting the loudspeaker in a closed box. We recall from Chapter 1 that when sound is reflected from parallel walls, a resonance condition is established with a frequency given by

$$f_{\text{resonance}} = \frac{v_s}{\lambda} = \frac{v_s}{2d} \tag{6.2}$$

where: v_s = velocity of sound
λ = wavelength
d = separation between parallel walls

A three-dimensional enclosure has many independent resonant frequencies. In Fig. 6.8 we see that the dimensions of the box determine the fundamental frequencies for modes with axes along the box edges. Each of these modes also has many harmonics. In addition, there are

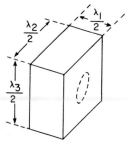

$\frac{\lambda_1}{2}$

$\frac{\lambda_2}{2}$

$\frac{\lambda_3}{2}$

Fig. 6.8. Diagram showing relation between three independent directions in rectangular box and three fundamental resonant wavelengths. In each case, separation between walls is half the wavelength.

resonant modes with axes oblique to the edges of the box. These modes are, in general, not harmonic.

These resonances can be destructive both mechanically and acoustically. Mechanically, large amplitude pressure waves built up at the resonant frequency can do severe damage to the fragile cone of the loudspeaker. Acoustically, the resonant waves can cause the sides of box to vibrate and act like diaphragms, creating large amplitude sound waves outside the box. To eliminate these resonant frequencies, manufacturers of loudspeaker enclosures often pack the empty space in the box with sound-absorbing material.

In some enclosures it is possible to use the low frequency sounds produced from the rear of the loudspeaker to support those sounds produced from the front. Figure 6.9 shows an enclosure with a port positioned so that sounds leaving the rear of the speaker will exit the port *inphase* with the next wave emanating from the front of the loudspeaker. This is possible if the path length is such that the rear wave is delayed by half of one period $(T/2)$. When the rear wave leaves the port, it is inphase with the wave from the front of the speaker (Fig. 6.10).

Note that this procedure will provide a boosted bass response for the loudspeaker-enclosure combination, since for these frequencies the wave from the port will add to the wave from the front of the loudspeaker. For other frequencies (with other wavelengths, of course) perhaps the port wave would not arrive inphase with the front wave. To handle this, one normally uses as packing material in the enclosure a substance that is highly absorbing for high frequencies but not absorbing for low frequencies. Thus, the low frequencies are passed to the port and emanated inphase. The high frequencies are absorbed and neither cause resonance problems nor out-of-phase port emission.

During the above discussion perhaps you stopped to calculate the effective bass boost frequency for a typical loudspeaker enclosure, say, about 1 m high. If the effective path length x in Fig. 6.9 is 0.75 m, then the maximum bass boost frequency will be

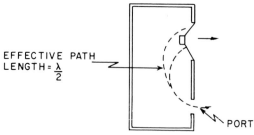

Fig. 6.9. Loudspeaker mounted in ported enclosure. Path length is such that sound from rear side of speaker leaves port inphase with sound from front.

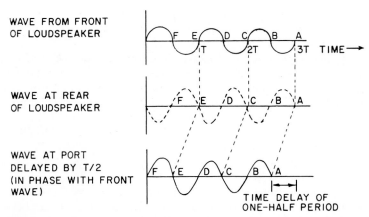

Fig. 6.10. Diagrams of waves at different points. Rear wave is always out of phase with front wave. By delaying rear wave a half period ($T/2$), wave at port is inphase with front wave (AB at port is inphase with BC from front).

$$f = \frac{\text{velocity of sound}}{\text{wavelength of boosted signal}} = \frac{v}{2x}$$

$$= \frac{345 \text{ m/s}}{2 \times 0.75 \text{ m}} = \frac{345}{1.5} \text{ Hz} = 230 \text{ c/s}$$

This frequency is surprisingly high and is not considered bass at all; to get true bass boost of a frequency, say, of 60 Hz would require a cabinet 4 m in height. We see that something different must be done to the cabinet to boost very low frequencies.

In practice two other approaches are used to get bass boost from a ported enclosure. The first method is to construct inside the speaker enclosure a labyrinth for the sound wave to follow—barricades around which the wave must bend to reach the port. The labyrinth is designed to increase the effective path length of travel of the wave.

The second method used to get bass boost is far more important than the technique of increasing path length. Thus far we have ignored this very important point: the phase difference between the waves from the front of the speaker and from the port depends on the acoustic impedance of the port. Recall from Chapter 4 that the phase of electrical signals depends on the electrical impedance of the elements (resistors, capacitors, inductors, etc.) through which the signals pass. In the same way, the phase of a pressure wave in air passing through an opening such as a loudspeaker port depends on the acoustic impedance of the opening. In fact, the response (amplitude and phase) of all electrical, mechanical, and acoustic systems depends on impedance.

We shall not discuss how acoustic impedance is employed in loudspeaker cabinets other than to say that most ported enclosures have a tube (either cylindrical or rectangular) attached to the port. The properties of this tube (length, cross-sectional area, how deep it protrudes into the cavity, smoothness of surface, etc.) determine the acoustic impedance of the opening. Since all waves that exit through the port must pass through the tube, the phase of these waves can be controlled. In practice the tube will be inserted and slowly moved in and out until the position of maximum reinforcement of the sound from the front of the speaker is achieved. This process is called tuning the port. Such loudspeaker cabinet designs are often called tuned port enclosures. Excellent books that discuss the how-to's of construction of ported enclosures may be found in the reading list at the back of the book.

Another interesting feature of an enclosed speaker is that the air pressure inside the box acts on the speaker cone. When the speaker cone moves inward, the pressure inside the box becomes higher than the atmospheric pressure; when the cone moves outward, the internal pressure drops below the atmospheric pressure. The result is that the difference in air pressure between the inside and outside adds an additional force to the speaker cone, resisting the motion of the cone. The air pressure acts in the same manner as the suspension around the outside of the speaker cone. Both resist the motion; both contribute to the spring constant k of the cone-suspension system. (Recall the discussion of Hooke's law in Chapter 1.) In fact, some speakers are designed to employ air pressure as the primary constituent in the suspension mechanism. These speakers are called air suspension systems.

Commercially available air suspension systems are usually produced from one design; that is, the speakers and the enclosures are designed to be one unit. The cabinets are tightly sealed to prevent air leaks, since any leaks will reduce the pressure inside the box and defeat the designed purposes of the system. (Usually one very small hole is present to allow the pressure inside the enclosure to adjust to changes in atmospheric pressure.) Clearly one should not tamper with cabinets of air suspension systems without confidence of successfully resealing the airtight seals!

6.4   BROAD FREQUENCY SPECTRUM SYSTEMS

We have discussed principles on which to base speaker design, enclosure design, and horn acoustic matching. Let us examine the practical problem of trying to produce all audio frequencies with a single transducer. Because we know that we must move large volumes of air for reproduction at low frequencies and only small volumes for high frequencies, we may expect that a single transducer might not be the most practical means of reproducing all audio frequencies. A 15-in diameter magnetic loudspeaker will produce low frequencies very well, but at high frequencies the cone vibration may cause small, isolated, local regions of the cone to begin to oscillate. The speaker will no longer behave as a single piston; different frequencies will be produced at different positions from the same cone. (This condition has been called cone breakup; besides being acoustically bad, this condition can damage or stretch the material of the cone itself.)

To eliminate these problems it is common to use a system of speakers—large ones for low frequencies and smaller ones for high frequencies. A typical system may have one 12-in bass woofer, one or two 6-in midrange speakers, and one or more 3-in tweeters for very high frequencies. To prevent the high frequency signals from even being sent to the bass speaker, a crossover network is used. This network is essentially an electrical signal filter. All frequencies come into the crossover network where the spectrum is filtered into separate bands for the individual low, medium, and high frequency transducers. Some overlap of these bands is allowed to produce a smooth transition between the various components (see Fig. 6.11).

6.5   SYSTEMS WITH SEVERAL IDENTICAL LOUDSPEAKERS

Let us examine the acoustical effects of driving two or more identical loudspeakers with the same signal at the same time. Suppose we position two speakers side by side as in Fig. 6.12. Suppose further that the two speakers are wired so that when the input signal is positive, both cones move outward; that is, they are inphase. At a point along a line perpendicular to the plane of the speakers and equally spaced from each, the resulting sound will be as follows. The amplitude of the resultant will be the sum of the amplitude of each wave (twice the amplitude of one speaker alone). Recall that intensity depends on the square of amplitude; thus the intensity of sound at position 1 in the drawing is four times the intensity from one speaker alone.

We have not created new energy, and consequently, there must be other positions where the intensity of the sound is less than that due to one speaker alone. Position 2 in the drawing is such a place. This position is nearer one speaker than the other; the sound from the distant speaker has to travel farther to reach position 2. Therefore, even though the waves from the two speakers were created inphase, they are out of phase when they reach position 2. If the difference in the two path lengths is one-half wavelength, the two waves will be exactly out of phase and will cancel each other, resulting in no amplitude, no intensity, and therefore no sound at position 2.

Note that other frequencies will still produce sound at position 2,

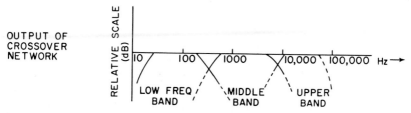

Fig. 6.11.   Crossover network output versus frequency.

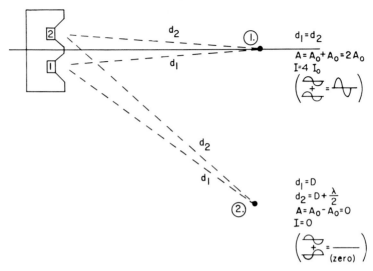

Fig. 6.12. Two identical speakers driven inphase.

since other frequencies have different wavelengths. Those frequencies will each have some other position where they cancel, appropriate to a $\lambda/2$ path difference for their wavelengths.

Note also that if the two speakers were wired improperly so that their waves moved exactly out of phase with each other, the intensity at position 1 would be zero and the intensity at position 2 would be four times the intensity due to one speaker alone.

If we connect three speakers so that they are driven inphase by the same signal, the amplitude along the perpendicular axis will be $A = A_0 + A_0 + A_0 = 3A_0$. (The speakers will each be the same distance from the point, and the three waves will arrive inphase.) Thus, the intensity will be nine times greater than that due to a single speaker. At other places the waves will arrive out of phase and cancel or be reduced.

Four speakers will produce four times the amplitude of one speaker, and sixteen times the intensity, on the perpendicular axis.

The useful result is that we may combine several (N) speakers in a single enclosure to produce the result shown in Fig. 6.13. In front of the N speakers the intensity is N^2 times that due to one speaker alone. Above and below the center line is very little sound radiation. To the sides the intensity is strong, since the side positions are equidistant from each of the individual speakers.

These speakers are termed column speakers. They are useful for sound reproduction in large auditoriums or out-of-doors, where any sound traveling in a vertical direction would be wasted. By using the interference of waves from multiple sources, the waves traveling vertically are eliminated, and the energy that is saved is directed toward

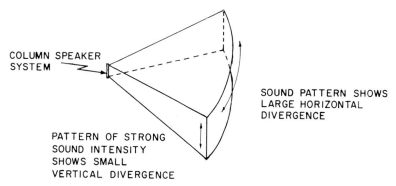

COLUMN SPEAKER
SYSTEM

SOUND PATTERN SHOWS
LARGE HORIZONTAL
DIVERGENCE

PATTERN OF STRONG
SOUND INTENSITY
SHOWS SMALL
VERTICAL DIVERGENCE

Fig. 6.13. Sound distribution from column speaker. Note narrow vertical and broad horizontal distribution.

the audience. In addition, the increase in intensity due to combined waves allows the user to reduce the volume of the amplifier. Therefore each single speaker will be required to produce less sound than if used alone. The result is that the travel (displacement) of the cones of each speaker is less than in single use, and consequently less distortion is produced.

6.6   SUMMARY

(1) To reproduce low frequency sounds at strong levels, it is necessary to move much greater volumes of air than to reproduce high frequency sounds at the same level. Thus, low frequency transducers must be large.

(2) Loudspeakers (transducers for converting electrical signals to acoustical signals) operate according to the same physical principles as microphones. Magnetic, electrostatic, and piezoelectric transducers are possible.

(3) Exponential horns may be used to improve the acoustical matching of a small speaker to a large room. Using a horn vastly increases the efficiency of energy transfer from the speaker into the room. Each horn has a low cutoff frequency below which the efficiency of energy transfer is severely decreased. The cutoff frequency is determined by the size of the horn.

(4) In open air the wave from the front of a speaker cone may cancel the wave from the rear of the cone (a problem mainly at low frequencies). Such cancellation may be prevented by mounting the speaker in a baffle.

(5) Mounting a speaker in a closed box can prevent the cancellation discussed in (4). However, new problems occur, since a box has its own natural resonant frequencies. Often sound-absorbing material is included in the enclosure to absorb the sound inside the box.

(6) A ported enclosure takes advantage of the sound inside the cabinet to reinforce the sound from the front of the speaker. The maximum reinforcement occurs for frequencies whose wavelength is twice the effective distance from the rear of the speaker to the port. Ported enclosures also employ acoustic impedance to control the phase of the wave exiting through the port. Often tubes are mounted in the port to determine the acoustic impedance.

(7) It is difficult to reproduce the entire frequency spectrum with one transducer. Commonly, the spectrum is divided into two or more regions of frequency, and specific transducers are installed for each of the various regions. The electrical network that divides the spectrum and routes the signals to the appropriate speaker is called a crossover network.

(8) When several speakers are driven with the same signal, interference occurs among the various waves that are created. The intensity at points where all the waves arrive inphase is $N^2 I_1$, where N is the number of speakers and I_1 is the intensity from one speaker. At other points the waves may cancel so effectively as to cause zero intensity for a particular frequency. Column speakers use the interference effects of multiple speakers to focus sound energy on a certain area (such as outdoor audiences) and eliminate the wasted sound energy sent to undesired listening areas (such as the sky in outdoor public address work).

QUESTIONS

1. Why are bass speakers large and high frequency speakers small?
2. Why are loudspeakers usually mounted in a baffle?
3. What is the purpose of using a horn on the end of a loudspeaker driver unit?
4. Why are exponential horns used much more widely for midrange speakers than for bass speakers?
5. What is the advantage of a ported (or vented) loudspeaker enclosure?
6. What is the effect of putting a tube in a port of an enclosure?
7. What is acoustic suspension?
8. How does the distribution pattern of a column speaker arrangement differ from the pattern of a single speaker? What causes this difference?
9. What are the meanings of "inphase" and "out of phase"?
10. Where does the energy that causes increased intensity at some points in the distribution pattern of a column speaker come from?

EXERCISES

1. How much air must be displaced each cycle in order to put out 10 acoustic W at 80 Hz? At 800 Hz? At 8000 Hz? (Answer: 10^3 cm³, etc.)
2. A small horn with a mouth opening of 25 cm is used in the reproduction of upper midrange frequencies. What is the lower frequency cutoff for this horn? (Answer: 345 Hz)

3. A build-it-yourself enthusiast constructs a ported, labyrinth speaker enclosure with an internal speaker-to-port distance of 4 ft (1.2 m). No tuning plug is included at the port. What low frequencies may be boosted by this system? How would one lower the effective range of the system?

4. Five identical speakers are arranged in column form and driven in-phase. If the intensity due to any one speaker is I_0, what is the intensity observed directly in front of the five speakers? (Answer: $25I_0$)

5. A column system containing identical, inphase speakers is measured to produce an intensity of 72×10^{-3} W/m². One speaker alone is known to produce 2×10^{-3} W/m². How many speakers are in the system?

6. A box has dimensions 1 m $\times$ 1.5 m $\times$ 0.5 m. Find at least three resonant frequencies for the air inside the box. (Answer: 173 Hz, etc.)

7
RADIO

One of the most interesting areas of sound reproduction involves radio transmission. In this chapter we discuss the nature of radio waves, suggest ways of producing and detecting radio signals, and examine both amplitude-modulated (AM) and frequency-modulated (FM) methods of signal transmission.

7.1 NATURE OF RADIO WAVES

One characteristic of radio waves is immediately apparent: radio waves do *not* require a medium for transmission. All the signals we have considered have required a medium in which to travel: sound waves move in some atomic medium such as air, electrical signals move in conductors, etc. (An electron beam does move through a vacuum in the vacuum tube, however.) Radio waves are different; they travel freely through a vacuum and also rather freely through some very dense materials such as glass or concrete. Radio waves are not disturbances of atoms or electrons but rather disturbances of fields. [These waves are composed simultaneously of changing electric (E) and magnetic (B) fields that are propagating through space.] In Fig. 7.1 we see a drawing of an electromagnetic wave at one instant. The oscillations of the electric field are at right angles to the oscillations of the magnetic field. The two fields are inphase; when E is maximum, B is also maximum. The direction of travel is to the right; some instant of time later the entire wave will be shifted to the right.

✳✳✳ [A second characteristic of these waves is that they seem to travel incredibly fast.] That is, if we are listening to a commercial radio station when the announcer gives the time, we notice that the time given always seems to agree with our time, even though the station is located in some distant city. It is as though the transmission of the radio signal were instantaneous. The speed of travel of radio waves has been measured very accurately and is known to be $2.998 \ldots \times 10^8$ m/s. For our purposes we may assume the speed to be 3×10^8 m/s.

This very high velocity indicates another difference of these radio waves from, say, sound waves. The speed of travel of sound in air is

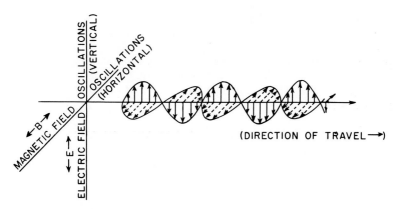

Fig. 7.1.   Instantaneous view of electromagnetic wave.

about 1130 ft/s $=$ 345 m/s.   Thus, a sound wave of frequency 100 Hz would have a wavelength of

$$\lambda = \frac{v_s}{f} = \frac{345 \text{ m/s}}{100 \text{ c/s}} = 3.45 \text{ m}$$

or about 11.3 ft.   On the other hand, a radio wave with a frequency of 100 Hz would have a wavelength of

$$\lambda = \frac{v_r}{f} = \frac{3 \times 10^8 \text{ m/s}}{100 \text{ c/s}} = 3 \times 10^6 \text{ m} = 3,000,000 \text{ m}$$

which is 1850 mi!   The speed of travel of radio waves is so much greater than the speed of sound that all our calculations take on different proportions.

Are there other electromagnetic waves than these we have called radio waves?   The answer is yes.   Radio, TV, light, X-ray, radar, and microwaves are all electromagnetic waves.   In fact, to call an electromagnetic wave "light" or "radio" is simply a convenience.   As shown in Fig. 7.2, all electromagnetic waves are the same phenomenon; labels are

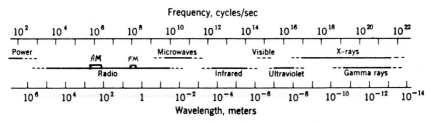

Fig. 7.2.   Electromagnetic spectrum.   (From David Halliday and Robert Resnick, *Fundamentals of Physics,* p. 654; © 1970, John Wiley and Sons, Inc., New York.   Used by permission.)

used to define waves that have a certain wavelength. The speed of travel of each of these waves has been measured; they all travel with the same speed, 3×10^8 m/s. This speed is normally called the speed of light and is denoted by the letter c.

Commercial radio in the United States includes the AM band: frequencies 535–1605 kHz, wavelengths 5.5–1.6 $\times$ 10^2 m; and the FM band: frequencies 88–108 MHz, wavelengths 3.4–2.8 m.

7.2 PRODUCTION AND DETECTION OF RADIO WAVES

Radio waves consist of oscillating electric and magnetic fields. In principle it is simple to produce such fields; we merely need to have an oscillating quantity of charge such as electrons. In Fig. 7.3 we see such a system; a long conductor is broken in the middle and connected to a source of voltage. The polarity of the source causes one end of the wire to become negative and the other end to become positive, and a charge accumulates on the wire and produces an electric field. Furthermore, as the process is developing, a current is flowing. These moving charges generate a magnetic field. The polarity of the source then changes, the electrons flow to the other end of the wire, and both the electric field and magnetic field reverse.

These fields travel through space with the speed of light. The alternating voltage source is ever changing: positive, negative, positive, negative, etc. Thus, the fields are ever changing, and the wave diagrammed in Fig. 7.1 is created.

(The above discussion is not intended to be and is not a complete description of the generation of electromagnetic waves. Electromagnetic theory is a rich and deep subject. Here we attempt to show that both electric and magnetic fields are generated by the motion and accumulation of charge.)

These waves may be detected in much the same manner: we allow the passing electromagnetic wave to influence electrons, and we detect that influence. In Fig. 7.4 we show another long conductor (or antenna) under the influence of a passing electromagnetic wave.

Only the electric field is shown to make the drawing more easily interpreted. The electric field at the conductor creates a force on the free electrons in the conductor pointing toward A and they flow through the detector to B. (Since electrons are negative, they flow in a direction opposite to the direction of the electric field itself.) As the field oscillates,

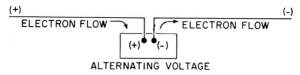

Fig. 7.3. Conductor connected to an alternating voltage source.

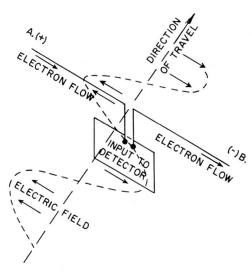

Fig. 7.4.   Influence of passing electromagnetic wave on conductor.

the current oscillates. When the field is strong the current is strong. The flow of electrons exactly reproduces, as a current, the frequency and amplitude characteristics of the electromagnetic wave.

Note that we may regard the influence on the electrons as creating an alternating voltage at the detector as well as an alternating current. Recall that voltage and current are related to each other by resistance. If the resistance of the detector is R, then Ohm's law gives the voltage at the input terminals of the detector to be $V = IR$, where I is the current we have been discussing. (Ohm's law is actually only literally valid for direct currents; in alternating currents the voltage and current may not be inphase with each other and Ohm's law must be modified. The significant point for discussion is that we may think of the influence of the electromagnetic wave on the electrons as creating either a current through or a voltage across the detector.)

7.3   SELECTION OF ONE SIGNAL

Let us consider further the influence on the free electrons in the conductor. Many electromagnetic waves are passing by the conductor at the same time. The free electrons are influenced by the electric fields of light, radar waves, and even cosmic rays. The result is that the voltage signal at the detector is a combination of all these input frequencies. Before we can consider transmission of audio information by radio waves, we must investigate means of selecting one signal out of the many that fall on the antenna.

There are many ways to select only one signal; some are quite sophisticated. We shall investigate one simple means because of the

basic physics it involves. We shall employ an electrical circuit with
electrical resonance as in Chapter 4. [When a signal having a frequency
near the resonant frequency enters the circuit, the circuit begins to oscillate and effectively amplifies that signal.] We all have heard acoustical
resonance; we blow across a pop bottle, and one sound emerges. Many
different frequencies are present in the blowing sounds from our lips
but only one sound is "amplified": that of the resonant frequency of
the air column in the pop bottle.

A simple electrical circuit that will demonstrate resonance consists
of just two components, a capacitor and an inductor. (In Chapter 4 we
discuss a resonant system having capacitance, inductance, and resistance.
We assume that the resistance is so small that we can ignore it.) Recall that an inductor is a coil of wire—effectively an electromagnet. The
property of inductance might be described as the property of a coil
that produces a magnetic field when a current flows through the coil.
For our discussion we may consider an inductor as a device that stores
energy in the form of a magnetic field; a capacitor stores energy as an
electric field.

The circuit is shown in Fig. 7.5 in five illustrations. We shall discuss
each step individually.

Step A: We start at the instant the capacitor is fully charged. Energy is stored in the electric field between the plates. No magnetic field
exists in the inductor because no current is flowing.

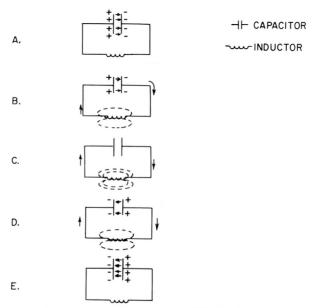

Fig. 7.5. Energy flow in a capacitor-inductor *(LC)* circuit.

Step B: The electrons now begin to flow from the negatively charged plate through the inductor to the positively charged plate. Some energy is still stored in the capacitor, since there are still some charges there. However, the flow of current now causes a magnetic field in the inductor, and some energy is being stored in that magnetic field.

Step C: At this instant the charge on the capacitor is zero; there is no energy stored in the capacitor. Current is still flowing, however, and all the energy of the circuit is stored in the strong magnetic field.

Step D: The magnetic field has begun to "collapse"; it is weakening and is feeding its stored energy back into the circuit in the form of recharging the capacitor. The loss of energy from the magnetic field is being stored as the energy of an electric field in the capacitor. Note that charge is still flowing.

Step E: The current has stopped; the magnetic field is zero. The capacitor is now fully charged, but with opposite polarity to that in Step A. Once again all the energy is stored in the capacitor.

Note that the final state of the circuit is identical to the initial state except for the change in the polarity of the capacitor charge. Thus the process will repeat with the current flowing in the opposite direction. This repeating will go on and on, which means that the circuit will oscillate. The frequency of oscillations of such a circuit is given by

$$f_0 = \frac{1}{2\pi}\sqrt{\frac{1}{LC}} \qquad (7.1)$$

where L is the inductance and C is the capacitance (see Chapter 4 on impedance). [From this equation we see that we can *change* the frequency of the circuit by changing either the inductance L or the capacitance C: we can "tune" the circuit.] * * *

This tunable resonant electrical circuit can be used to select one signal from the many electromagnetic wave signals incident on an antenna. All the signals are fed to the LC circuit; any signal with a frequency near the resonant frequency will cause the circuit to begin to oscillate. [This signal will grow in amplitude because of resonance while the others will not.] In fact, the LC circuit will effectively "short out" many of the other signals. The very low frequency signals will pass through the inductor; and the very high frequency signals will pass through the capacitor, as discussed in Section 3.4.2. If this circuit is connected to an amplifier, only those frequencies near the resonant frequency will be strong at the amplifier input. Thus, we have selected those frequencies near the resonant frequency of our LC circuit and rejected all others (see Fig. 7.6).

7.4 AMPLITUDE-MODULATED RADIO SIGNALS

Having discussed methods of creating and detecting electromagnetic waves, we turn now to methods of passing information via those waves.

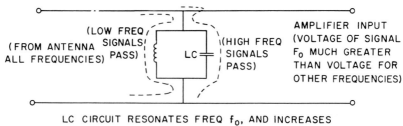

LC CIRCUIT RESONATES FREQ f_0, AND INCREASES
VOLTAGE OF THAT SIGNAL

Fig. 7.6. Use of *LC* circuit resonance to amplify signal of resonant frequency
f_0 while shorting other signals.

For our purposes we shall only consider audio information transmission,
although the principles may be extended to other types of transmission
such as television.

Amplitude modulation is one method of superimposing audio information on electrical signals used to generate electromagnetic waves.
The process is as follows. A very high frequency signal of constant frequency and amplitude is produced in a device called an oscillator. This
carrier signal is fed into a modulator unit that is controlled by some
audio input. When the audio signal has a maximum, the amplitude of
the high frequency signal is increased; when the audio signal has a minimum, the amplitude of the high frequency signal is decreased (see Figs.
7.7. and 7.8).

✳ ✳ ✳ [The amplitude-modulated signal is then amplified and eventually
sent to an antenna.] In the antenna the signal causes a flow of electrons
which in turn generates electromagnetic waves. The frequency of the
waves will be the same as the very high frequency carrier signal, and
the amplitude of the waves will be determined by the audio information.

Note in Fig. 7.8 that when the modulation is greater than 100%,
the original high frequency signal is simply cut off for some period of

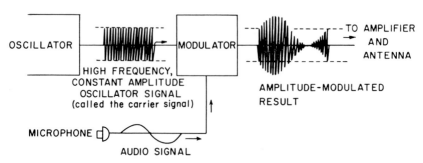

Fig. 7.7. Block diagram of amplitude modulation system. Illustration shows
100% modulation: amplitude of modulated signal varies from $A = 0$ to $A = 2A_{\text{oscillator}}$.

A. LESS THAN 100%
   MODULATION:

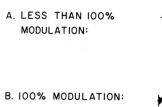

B. 100% MODULATION:

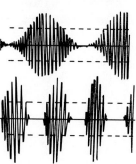

C. GREATER THAN
   100% MODULATION:
   (OVER MODULATION)

Fig. 7.8.   Three cases of degree of amplitude modulation.

time. Case C represents obvious distortion since the waveform does not coincide with the input audio signal. Thus, commercial radio broadcasting is limited to the 100% modulation case, which is in effect a limit on the dynamic range of the audio information transmitted.

A general result of the mathematical analysis of amplitude modulation is that the resulting wave can be thought of as being composed of three signals. To illustrate this, suppose that the high frequency carrier signal is of frequency f_0 and the audio signal is of frequency f. The modulated result will appear as diagrammed in the previous drawings. However, the same result would have been obtained if we had added together signals of the following frequencies (with certain appropriate amplitudes):

Signal one: frequency f_0
Signal two: frequency $f_0 + f$ (upper sideband)
Signal three: frequency $f_0 - f$ (lower sideband)

We may add these together to produce a result identical with the modulated signal, or we may take the modulated signal and analyze it into these three components!

Signal two $(f_0 + f)$ is called the upper sideband, and signal three $(f_0 - f)$ is called the lower sideband. These sidebands are very important; they carry all the audio information. The basic carrier signal is effectively untouched. All the energy or power involved in the modulation process is stored in the generation of the sideband frequencies.

Consider a station for which the carrier frequency is $f_0 = 1000$ kHz. When amplitude-modulated by an audio signal of frequency 1 kHz (1000 Hz), the result is a signal composed of the three frequencies: 1000 kHz,

1001 kHz, and 999 kHz, corresponding to the carrier, the upper sideband, and the lower sideband. If the audio signal were 10 kHz, the resulting amplitude-modulated signal would be composed of 1000 kHz, 1010 kHz, and 990 kHz. In other words, the AM signal occupies a band of frequencies from $f_0 - f$ (990 kHz) to $f_0 + f$ (1010 kHz). The width of the band is 2f, twice the audio frequency.

We now see a possible problem from this sideband production due to amplitude modulation. If two stations have carrier frequencies separated by, say, 10 kHz, then the maximum audio frequency transmitted by either would be 5 kHz. A higher audio frequency would cause the band of one station to overlap the band of the other station, and distortion would result.

The Federal Communications Commission (FCC) which regulates broadcasting has imposed limits on the maximum audio frequency that a station may transmit. With a few exceptions, public AM broadcasting is limited to an upper audio frequency of 5 kHz. Thus, each AM station occupies a band of 10 kHz in the AM region of the electromagnetic spectrum. We saw in Fig. 7.2 that the frequency range for AM radio was 535 kHz to 1605 kHz. The width of the spectrum is then 1070 kHz, which divides into approximately 107 bands of 10 kHz each, meaning 107 available frequency slots for stations in a given area. Actually, the FCC requires a normal separation between stations of 20 kHz. This separation allows for a 10-kHz gap between the bands of adjacent stations, preventing accidental overlap and reducing the strict requirements of excellent selectivity on the radio set used to receive the broadcast. The 20-kHz separation between stations reduces the available frequency slots to about 50 in a given listening area.

In summary, we have seen that an audio signal may be used to control the amplitude of some constant frequency carrier wave. Two sidebands are produced above and below the carrier frequency, causing the final AM wave to occupy a band of frequencies centered on the carrier frequency. Two disadvantages of AM broadcasting arise: the bandwidth limits the number of stations that may broadcast simultaneously without mutual interference, and the 100% modulation criterion limits the dynamic range of the audio signals transmitted. Furthermore, the FCC has chosen to limit AM broadcasting to a rather poor frequency range of 0–5 kHz in order to decrease the bandwidth and allow more stations to operate.

7.5 FREQUENCY-MODULATED RADIO SIGNALS

The origin of the signal used in frequency-modulated (FM) broadcasting is in principle no different from the origin of the signal for AM work: the original signal comes from an oscillator. In fact, if no audio signal is present, the AM and FM results are identical; it is only the methods of modulation that differ between the two. In frequency modulation, the actual frequency of the carrier wave changes while the amplitude is held constant. The number of times per second that the carrier frequency changes above and below f_0 is determined by the frequency of the audio input. The amount of deviation of the carrier from f_0 is determined by the amplitude of the audio signal. Thus, in FM the signal again occupies a band of frequencies centered about the original carrier frequency f_0 (see Fig. 7.9).

Note that no intrinsic limit to dynamic range is imposed by the physics. In AM there is a limit caused by the 100% modulation criterion; a louder audio signal would drive the system to modulation greater than 100% and cause inevitable distortion. In FM we may use very loud audio signals, which only cause the frequency of the wave to deviate farther and farther from the original carrier frequency f_0. There of course are practical limits to the deviation from frequency f_0. [For example, the FCC has imposed a deviation limit of ± 75 kHz so that the allowed bandwidth per channel will be sufficiently wide to provide adequate dynamic range and yet small enough to allow many stations to broadcast in the FM region of the spectrum.] In addition to the ± 75 kHz, the FCC requires a guard band of ± 25 kHz to minimize any interference problems, so that each station occupies a bandwidth of 200 kHz, centered about its original carrier frequency.

Of the many ways to illustrate information storage in an FM signal, a method as shown in Fig. 7.10 is useful. Note that the frequency range for the audio information may be as high as 15 kHz. (Compare the 5-

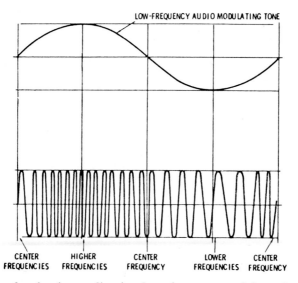

Fig. 7.9. Result of using audio signal to frequency-modulate signal. (From Leonard Feldman, *FM from Antenna to Audio*, 1969, Sams, Indianapolis, p. 10. Reprinted by permission.)

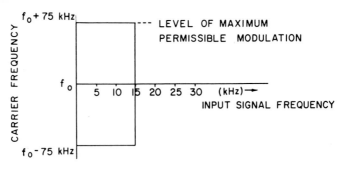

Fig. 7.10. Diagram showing allowed frequency-modulation deviation (vertical axis) and audio input signal (horizontal axis) in monophonic FM system. (Adapted from Leonard Feldman, *FM Multiplexing for Stereo,* 1972, Sams, Indianapolis. Used by permission.)

kHz upper limit for AM.) Also, the $\pm$75-kHz frequency variation would correspond to the loudest (greatest amplitude) signal allowed by the FCC. All softer (less amplitude) signals would cause a frequency deviation of less than 75 kHz from the central frequency f_0 (the station frequency).

7.5.1 Demodulation of FM Signals

Now that we have investigated how an audio signal may be used to modulate the frequency of a signal, may we demodulate that signal to recover the audio information? Several methods are possible; we will discuss one simple method that applies physical principles we have already treated.

We allow the FM signal to drive two resonant LC circuits, circuit A tuned above the carrier frequency f_0, circuit B tuned below f_0. Suppose the two inductors, L_A and L_B, are parts of a transformer system as shown in Fig. 7.11. When the FM frequency deviates above f_0, resonance will occur in circuit A and a large output will be caused. When the FM frequency deviates below f_0, resonance will occur in circuit B, and large output will result. Suppose we change the polarity of the output of circuit B, making it negative with respect to circuit A. Thus, when A is resonant, the output will be positive; when B is resonant, the output will be negative (see Fig. 7.12).

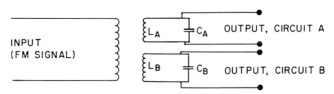

Fig. 7.11. Two LC resonant circuits driven by one FM input signal.

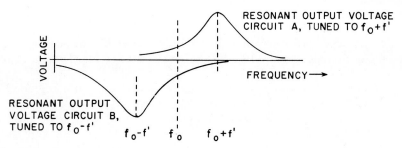

Fig. 7.12. Resonant voltages of two *LC* circuits tuned above and below center frequency f_0.

The deviations of the FM signal have been transformed into a voltage signal that alternates from positive to negative. The amplitude of this signal depends on the deviation in frequency of the original FM input. The frequency of the voltage output oscillations is determined by the number of times per second that the FM signal deviates above and below f_0, that is, the number of times circuit A is excited to make the output positive and B is excited to produce the negative output. [We have therefore reclaimed both the frequency and amplitude information of the original audio signal.] ◄— ✷✷✷

7.5.2 Application of Stereo Information to FM Signals

Thus far our discussion has concerned the superposition of one set of audio information onto an FM signal. Let us consider now the common method of superimposing two independent sets of information onto one FM signal.➔ The method is known as multiplexing and involves some type of encoding procedure during transmission as well as decoding at the receiver. ◄—✷✷✷

Consider first that if we have two audio signals L and R (left and right) we may encode and decode these signals in the following manner. Let us electronically form the sum and difference of these.

Sum: signal L + signal R = new signal $(L + R)$
Difference: signal L — signal R = new signal $(L - R)$

The new signals carry all the information of the old signals, albeit in a new form. We can completely recover the old signals by again performing electronic summing:

Sum: $(L + R) + (L - R) = 2L$
Difference: $(L + R) - (L - R) = 2R$

Our original signals are recovered with the results of left-only and right-only information. ◄——— ✷✷✷

In stereo multiplexing of FM, this procedure is performed. The

$(L + R)$ signal is broadcast in a manner identical to the methods we have discussed. Thus all monophonic FM receivers will reproduce this $(L + R)$ signal, which contains both sets of stereo information. The monophonic systems reproduce all the music but not in separated stereo form.

The second signal $(L - R)$ is treated in a manner not reproduced on monophonic sets. This signal is used to amplitude-modulate a 38-kHz signal. The result of this process produces the following: the carrier, 38 kHz; the upper sideband, 38 kHz $+ (L - R)$; and the lower sideband, 38 kHz $- (L - R)$. Because the $(L - R)$ signal contains audio frequencies of 50 Hz to 15,000 Hz, we see that the sidebands will extend from 23,000 Hz to 37,950 Hz [lower sideband $= 38$ kHz $- (L - R)$] and from 38,050 Hz to 53,000 Hz (upper sideband). Recall from our discussion of sideband formation that the carrier itself is undisturbed and does not carry any audio information. Thus, in FM broadcasting, the frequency signal between 37,950 Hz and 38,050 Hz is suppressed. It serves no useful function and is removed. The remaining sideband signals are then also used to frequency-modulate the carrier, just as the $(L + R)$ signal was used.

Realize that when the signal is received, the 38,000 Hz region that was suppressed must be re-added before demodulation can be accomplished. Rather than depending on each receiver to provide this signal, all FM stereo stations broadcast another signal, called a pilot tone, of 19 kHz. The receiver multiplies this by two to get the 38-kHz signal necessary for recombination with the $(L - R)$ sidebands before demodulation. The pilot tone provides not only a perfect frequency match for receiver and transmitter, but also provides a perfect phase match.

The final signal is shown in Fig. 7.13. Note that the pilot tone, which is always present in stereo broadcasting, requires 10% of the available modulation range. Thus, the total modulation range possible for the audio portion must be reduced to provide some portion of the allotment to the pilot signal. Another way to view the problem is that we have a certain allowed amount of information available (maximum modulation corresponding to maximum dynamic range). If we try to add more

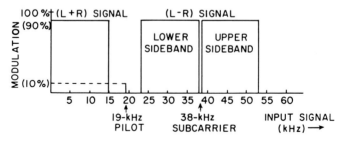

Fig. 7.13. Final modulation and input frequency spectrum for stereo multiplexed FM signal.

information, we must either increase the allotment or decrease the previous amount of information (reduce the dynamic range).

✳✳ ⌈In accomplishing stereo broadcasting, something is lost: the dynamic range available in monophonic broadcasting has been reduced to allow for the pilot tone.⌉ Further, both monophonic and stereophonic broadcasting stations may supplement their income by providing a third signal for background music purposes. These signals are allowed by the FCC through the Subsidiary Communications Act (SCA) to support FM broadcasting at a time when FM work was not economically rewarding. The stations incorporate the SCA information as a third-signal amplitude modulated onto a carrier of 67 kHz, using this result to frequency-modulate the main carrier signal. The station then leases specially designed receivers to businesses that wish to have uninterrupted background music. The SCA signals, limited to 10% of available modulation capability, provide another decrease in the main audio signal dynamic range. The resulting signal is illustrated in Fig. 7.14.

7.6   NOISE IN AM AND FM RADIO SYSTEMS

Why can lightning and other electrical disturbances cause such offensive noise on AM radios while not creating much noise on FM? An electric spark (any electric spark) is a charge accelerated by large electric fields and decelerated by collision with air molecules. (The bright glow of an electric spark is mostly due to very hot air.) These tremendous accelerations of charge radiate electromagnetic waves as discussed in Section 7.2. What frequencies are these waves? All frequencies result from such a spark discharge, since so many charges are accelerated and since the accelerations are not the same for the various charges.

The electromagnetic waves produced by a spark are just like the waves produced by a radio transmitter (all electromagnetic waves are alike), but they do not contain audio information. That is, the spark discharge radiation is random rather than having either periodic amplitude or frequency modulation. These waves propagate in space as do waves carrying signals; they cause electrons to flow in antennas as do desired waves. What happens in an AM receiver and an FM receiver when such a wave passes an antenna?

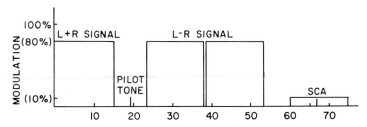

Fig. 7.14.   FM signal with stereo multiplexing, pilot tone, and one SCA channel.

First, the AM radio. In Section 7.3 we discuss how an LC circuit can distinguish one frequency radio wave from another and select one signal for amplification. That discrimination is based on the different frequencies of the two signals. Each of us has experienced the case (usually about sundown) when two stations on the same frequency are received and cannot be separated because of the type of selection process of the LC circuit: simple resonance. Now, if a noise signal from a spark contains all frequencies, it must contain the frequency f_0 of the LC circuit. Consequently, the LC circuit passes the noise just as it does the desired signal. Once into the amplifier, the noise signal is treated as any other. Because the noise signal is not periodic (even though it may have amplitude variation), it produces a crackling sound rather than a tone in the loudspeaker. Thus AM radio techniques are susceptible to electromagnetic noise. ◄───── ✳ ✳ ✳

Now the FM radio. In Section 7.5.1 we discussed a simple detection system for FM radiation. The key to the selection of FM signals is the periodic change of frequency of the signal. Spark discharges do not generate periodically varying frequency waves. Waves of different frequencies do exist but in most cases they are generated almost simultaneously. Thus, if one wave excites circuit A in Figs. 7.11 and 7.12, another will excite circuit B at the same time. Since the output voltage of B is opposite in sign to the output of A, the two tend to cancel each other out; FM techniques are not susceptible to electromagnetic noise. ◄───✳✳✳

7.7   SUMMARY

(1)   Radio waves are varying electric and magnetic fields that travel through space at the speed of light, 3×10^8 m/s.

(2)   The electromagnetic spectrum includes all types of electromagnetic waves arranged by their frequencies. "Light," "radio," etc., are convenient names for the waves in different regions of the spectrum, but all types of waves are actually the same phenomenon.

(3)   Electromagnetic waves may be created by imposing an alternating voltage on the center of a split wire. The accumulation of charge on the ends of the wire creates an electric field, and the flow of charge in the wire creates a magnetic field.

(4)   An electromagnetic wave may be detected by exposing a wire to the wave, and observing the flow of electrons in the wire. (The wire may be any conducting material.)

(5)   An inductance-capacitance (LC) circuit is one simple means of separating one signal from the many signals received by an antenna. The LC circuit exhibits an electrical resonance at a well-defined frequency. Signals of that particular frequency are boosted in amplitude by the resonance circuit.

(6)   Amplitude modulation is the process of using one signal (audio) to control the amplitude of another signal known as the carrier. A result of the process is that sidebands are produced, signals whose frequencies

are above or below the carrier frequency. The AM signal has a bandwidth determined by the maximum audio frequency transmitted. To reduce the bandwidths and thereby to prevent stations from overlapping and interfering, the FCC has imposed a 0–5 kHz frequency range for AM modulation. A further AM disadvantage comes from the 100% modulation limit beyond which distortion ensues, thus limiting the dynamic range available in AM broadcasting.

(7) Frequency modulation is the process of using one signal (audio) to control the frequency of another signal. The magnitude of deviation of frequency from the base frequency f_0 carries the amplitude information of the audio signal. The number of times per second that the frequency deviates carries the frequency information of the audio signal.

(8) Two resonant circuits tuned above and below the base frequency f_0 may be used to demodulate FM signals. As the frequency of the FM signal varies above and below f_0, the two circuits are alternately excited. Both the amplitude and frequency of the audio signal are reclaimed.

(9) Multichannel information may be imposed on FM signals by using the signals to amplitude-modulate other high frequency carrier frequencies. Then each signal is added into one signal that frequency-modulates the base signal. (Normally the high frequency carrier signals are suppressed and not transmitted. A low intensity pilot tone that provides accurate frequency and phase information for the demodulation process is transmitted.)

(10) To ensure that monophonic FM receivers will not receive only part of the audio information, multichannel signals are mutiplexed; that is, two signals A and B are transmitted as $(A + B)$ and $(A - B)$. The monophonic receivers are designed to receive the $(A + B)$ signal that contains all the audio information. Stereo receivers translate both the $(A + B)$ and $(A - B)$ signals into their original, independent A and B forms. An SCA (background music) signal may also be multiplexed into the final transmitted signal.

(11) As the amount of information included in the single FM signal is increased, the dynamic range available is reduced.

(12) Amplitude-modulated radios are susceptible to noise due to electrical sparks, since sparking produces electromagnetic waves of all frequencies; FM radios are not very susceptible to spark noise, because FM receivers sense only periodic frequency variations in the electromagnetic waves. Sparks do not produce such periodic variations.

QUESTIONS

1. A radio wave passes by a backyard wire fence. The path of travel is perpendicular to the fence. Can the radio wave have any effect on the fence? If yes, what? If no, why not?
2. Describe a radio wave. What is it "made" of? In what ways is a radio wave like a light wave?

3. What does amplitude modulation mean? Can a sound wave be amplitude-modulated, or is AM a phenomenon only applicable to radio waves?

4. What does frequency modulation mean? Can any wave be frequency-modulated?

5. Why is the frequency range of audio information for most AM stations limited to 50–5000 Hz?

6. Why would increasing capacitance lower the resonant frequency of an LC circuit?

7. How can one radio signal carry two independent sets of information? (Describe the methods for putting stereo signals onto a radio wave.)

8. What is the function of the pilot tone used in FM broadcasting?

9. Why is FM reception not very sensitive to atmospheric electrical noise?

10. Explain why so little dynamic range is heard in the background music in medical offices and other places where SCA broadcasting techniques are used.

EXERCISES

1. A radio station is broadcasting at a frequency of 600 kHz. What is the wavelength of the radio wave? (Answer: 500 m)

2. A radio wave from a commercial radio station in the United States is known to have a wavelength of 3 m. What is the operating frequency of the station? Is it AM or FM?

3. An LC circuit having C equal to 2 μF is known to have a resonant frequency of 10^4 Hz. If C is increased to 8 μF, what will be the new resonant frequency?

4. If we reduce the inductance in an LC circuit to one-fourth its original value, what will happen to the resonant frequency?

5. A radio wave of frequency 600 kHz is amplitude-modulated by a 5-kHz tone. What signals are present in the transmitted wave? (Answer: 595 kHz, 600 kHz, etc.)

6. Suppose an FM station broadcasts on a center frequency of 1000 MHz (MHz stands for megahertz, or 10^6 Hz). If we measure the instantaneous frequency of the signal, we would probably find it to be different from 1000 MHz. Which of the following signal frequencies will correspond to the loudest audio information for that signal: (a) 999.25 MHz, (b) 999.75 MHz, (c) 1000 MHz, (d) 1000.25 MHz, or (e) 1000.50 MHz?

7. Using the FCC allowed bandwidth for FM broadcasting and the frequency band limits for commercial operation, calculate the number of FM channels available in any one area.

8
QUADRAPHONIC SYSTEMS

We have examined several techniques for multichannel information storage: two-channel grooves in discs; two-channel plus SCA background music signals on FM broadcasts; and the versatile multichannel, discrete tracks on magnetic tape. In this chapter we discuss quadraphonic storage and transmission and the associated problems with discs and FM. The treatment is intentionally condensed because we have already considered many of the principles that are needed. The technological means necessary to make the systems perform to maximum capability are beyond the scope of this book, and interested readers are encouraged to examine Leonard Feldman's book, *Four Channel Sound* (see reading list), which addresses both the techniques and limitations of four-channel systems.

8.1 MOTIVATION FOR FOUR-CHANNEL SOUND

Imagine yourself as a listener in the best seat in the house at a symphony orchestra performance. What do you hear? Of course, you hear sounds directly from the orchestra. But also you hear sounds reflected from every surface of the building. This reflected sound has been "colored" by the building; that is, as the sound reverberates around the room, the sound interacts with the walls of the room For instance, high frequency waves may be absorbed while low frequencies are reflected. Certainly some halls have poor acoustical properties and produce displeasing coloration of the sound, while other halls actually seem to make the sound more exciting.

How can we record the orchestra and the characteristics of the hall in which a performance is given? One way would be to put several microphones at one position in the room, all pointing in different directions to sense the sound from the various parts of the room. These sets of information could then be mixed to create one signal containing both orchestral and reverberation sounds.

Now let us play this information back over a one-channel, one-speaker system as shown in Fig. 8.1. We hear all the sound from one source, one localized point. The reverberation of the hall appears to originate from the same physical place as the orchestral sound. The

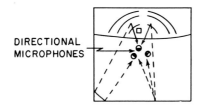
DIRECTIONAL
MICROPHONES
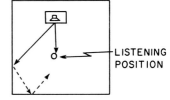
LISTENING
POSITION

Fig. 8.1. Left drawing: sketch of method of recording direct orchestral and reverberant sound at one position in auditorium. Right drawing: single-channel playback of same recorded signal in acoustically dead room.

sense of spaciousness of the hall has been lost, and the coloration of the sound by the hall has been changed.

Stereo (two-channel) reproduction restores much of the original spatial information (see Fig. 8.2). Certainly it is possible to recreate the spatial characteristics of, say, an orchestra and reproduce the violins on the left, the woodwinds in the center, the basses on the right, etc. However, it is not so easy to reproduce the spatial effect of the hall. The reverberation may be apparent in the recorded sound but again appears to be produced from the same position as the instruments themselves. Some characteristics of the hall are audible but the acoustical effect leading to the feeling of actually attending the performance is not there.

Four-channel reproduction offers such acoustic possibilities. Both the spatial arrangement of the instruments and the characteristics of the hall may be recorded and reproduced (see Fig. 8.3).

Note that four-channel systems offer new possibilities in music composition. As well as new special-effect acoustic phenomena, new music can be composed for unusual instrumental locations. For example, a recording engineer can change the acoustic placement of an instrument or soloist by shifting the channel on which the instrument is recorded. When played back, the instrument will appear to move around the room as the music progresses. Although these effects are not appropriate for classical music, they are a new and creative medium for popular music.

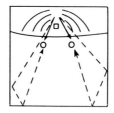
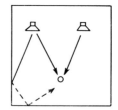

Fig. 8.2. Left drawing: two-channel (stereo) recording of orchestra and reverberant sound. Right drawing: two-channel reproduction.

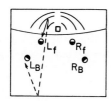 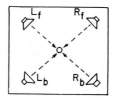

Fig. 8.3. Left drawing: four-channel recording of orchestra and reverberant sound. Symbols L and R refer to left and right; f and b refer to front and back. Right drawing: four-channel reproduction.

Four-channel reproduction is not the ultimate. The sound in the concert hall did not originate from four points, but from every part of every reflecting surface in the room. For example, the four channels may give a realistic and accurate illusion of the spatial quality of the sound horizontally, but they do not reproduce any spatial effect due to the vertical room structure. (Granted, this is a small point. It is intended to help the reader understand the difficulty of reproducing a "best seat in the house" concert situation.) Further, even if the speaker-amplifier arrangement is perfectly balanced for the listening position X in Fig. 8.4, the same arrangement will be unbalanced for position Y. To a listener at Y, the right-hand speakers will appear too loud because the sound field from the four sources is not uniform.

Why, then, four channels when surely forty, say, will produce a more uniform sound field, perhaps with floor and ceiling speakers to reproduce the three-dimensional spatial characteristics of the hall? Recall that each channel must have its own amplifiers and its own transducers, and that we must be able to store all the channels in a convenient manner. Four channels appear to be the economically and technically practical solution to the problems of keeping costs down while providing realistic reproduction of spatial characteristics.

Finally, note that having four independent original channels is *not* the only way to recover the room reverberation characteristics of the sound. A simple system that adds two speakers (and nothing more)

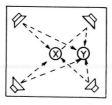

Fig. 8.4. Listening positions for four-channel reproduction. If the system is balanced for position X, a listener at Y will hear unbalanced sound.

to an existing stereo system can be used to recover some of the out-of-phase information on present stereo discs. Such systems are useful for improving present systems but do not allow the new composition potential of four-channel information. Interested readers are again referred to Feldman, *Four Channel Sound*.

8.2   FOUR-CHANNEL DISCS

Two ways to produce four-channel discs are: the discrete method, in which the four sets of information are kept separate, and the matrixing method, in which the four sets are mixed and later decoded.

8.2.1   Discrete Approach

How are four independent sets of information put into a single groove on a disc? We have seen from the discussion of stereo cartridges in Section 5.1.3 that the stylus moves in only two independent planes separated by 90°. Utilizing pickup coils rotated by 90° we are able to reproduce two sets of information independently. To put four channels into the two independent motions of the groove, we use a means similar to that used to put two channels into one FM-stereo radio signal.

For the moment, let us consider the left-front (L_f) and left-back (L_b) information and examine how these two independent channels may be stored with one motion of the record groove. We first form two new signals made of the sum and difference of L_f and L_b. We then record $(L_f + L_b)$ just as we did the conventional left stereo channel; $(L_f + L_b)$ is stored on the record in that form, undisturbed. At the same time we record the $(L_f - L_b)$ signal in the following way: (1) Generate a 30-kHz carrier signal. (2) Use the $(L_f - L_b)$ signal to *frequency-modulate* the 30-kHz carrier. (3) Add this new modulated carrier signal to the previous $(L_f + L_b)$ signal, and record both into the same motion of the groove (see Fig. 8.5).

On playback we must be able to recover the two sets of information, but that is rather easy to do (assuming the stylus can track the groove properly). In Fig. 8.6 a system is shown that separates the low frequency $(L_f + L_b)$ signal from the high frequency (30 kHz modulated by $L_f - L_b$) signal and then demodulates the $(L_f - L_b)$ information. Finally, the two signals are added and subtracted to recover L_f and L_b as pure, independent signals as in Section 7.5.2:

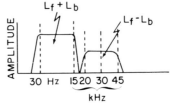

Fig. 8.5.   Method for putting two sets of information into one channel.

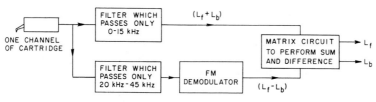

Fig. 8.6.   Recovering two signals from one track.

Sum: $[(L_f - L_b) + (L_f + L_b)]/2 = L_f$
Difference: $[(L_f - L_b) - (L_f + L_b)]/2 = L_b$

The right front (R_f) and right back (R_b) signals are treated similarly and recorded with the other independent motion of the groove.

Many features of this system are desirable; the most important feature is that the four channels L_f, L_b, R_f, and R_b are maintained as independent (discrete) entities. Furthermore, such a system is compatible with existing stereophonic systems since the present left channel will reproduce both L_f and L_b (the $L_f + L_b$ signal is stored in that form) and the present right channel will reproduce both R_f and R_b. The spatial characteristics only available in four channels have been lost, but all the acoustic signals are reproduced.

The chief disadvantages are technological. Conventional stereo recording cutters and reproducing cartridges were not designed to have flat response up to 45 kHz. Both the design of the reproducing stylus and the cutting techniques had to be revised. Appropriate cartridges have been produced and are commercially available. Also, typical materials for discs do not wear well at very high frequencies. New materials must be developed to provide reliable, long-life, four-channel storage.

This technique could, in principle, be used to put many channels into a single record groove. Technologically, this means going to much higher frequencies, and we must make tremendous technological advances before many-channel storage will be feasible.

8.2.2   Matrixing Method

The matrixing method is another means of putting four channels of information into the two independent motions of a groove of a disc. The name "matrix" comes from the basis of the technique: the mathematical method (known as matrix algebra) for solving several equations simultaneously. We will not actually perform matrix algebra operations here, but it is useful to recall a result from high school algebra that follows from the matrixing approach. If we have two unknown algebraic quantities x and y (or L and R in a stereo signal), we can find their values by knowing two different equations. For four unknowns such as L_f, L_b, R_f, and R_b, we need four different equations. Suppose we have two equations in four unknowns. We cannot solve for the independent four unknowns, but we can solve for combinations of the unknowns such as $(L_f + L_b)$ and $(R_f + R_b)$.

The matrixing approach to recording is to mix the four channels L_f, L_b, R_f, and R_b into two signals in such a way that even though the four cannot be reclaimed independently, convenient combinations may be reclaimed. Several manufacturers have employed the matrix approach to recording, and at this writing several different methods of mixing and reclaiming the signals are used. We shall discuss one basic approach that is relatively easy to understand. This method was the first to be demonstrated (by Peter Scheiber, the originator) and although it is not used presently, it will serve as a representative example of the technique. Scheiber suggested the four independent signals L_f, L_b, R_f, and R_b be combined and recorded in the following way:

$$L_{\text{total}} = 0.92 \ L_f + 0.92 \ L_b + 0.38 \ R_f - 0.38 \ R_b$$
$$R_{\text{total}} = 0.38 \ L_f - 0.38 \ L_b + 0.92 \ R_f + 0.92 \ R_b$$

It is easy to perform this combination. For example, if the microphone-preamplifier system for each channel has a volume control, we "turn down" the amplitude of the L_f signal to $0.92 \ L_f$ and the R_f signal to $0.38 \ R_f$. The only difficulty is to make the $0.38 \ R_b$ signal in L_{total} to be negative. Electronically this is also easy to do with a simple circuit called a *phase inverter*. If a positive voltage comes into the inverter, a negative voltage is put out. The common-emitter transistor circuit in Fig. 3.13 is a phase-inverting circuit.

Let us now consider how we may reclaim useful well-separated audio information from the above combinations of signals. Scheiber suggested the following set of equations for playback:

$$L_f' = 0.92 \ L_{\text{total}} + 0.38 \ R_{\text{total}}$$
$$L_b' = 0.92 \ L_{\text{total}} - 0.38 \ R_{\text{total}}$$
$$R_f' = 0.38 \ L_{\text{total}} + 0.92 \ R_{\text{total}}$$
$$R_b' = -0.38 \ L_{\text{total}} + 0.92 \ R_{\text{total}}$$

The primes indicate that the new, reclaimed signals are not the same as the original recorded signals. To illustrate this, let us solve R_f' equation, for example.

$$
\begin{aligned}
R_f' &= 0.38 \ L_{\text{total}} + 0.92 \ R_{\text{total}} \\
&= 0.38[0.92 \ L_f + 0.92 \ L_b + 0.38 \ R_f - 0.38 \ R_b] \\
&\quad + 0.92[0.38 \ L_f - 0.38 \ L_b + 0.92 \ R_f + 0.92 \ R_b] \\
&= (0.35 \ L_f + 0.35 \ L_b + 0.15 \ R_f - 0.15 \ R_b) \\
&\quad + (0.35 \ L_f - 0.35 \ L_b + 0.85 \ R_f + 0.85 \ R_b) \\
R_f' &= 0.7 \ L_f + R_f + 0.7 \ R_b
\end{aligned}
$$

The new R_f' signal is a combination of the original L_f, R_f, and R_b signals. The other equations may be solved to yield similar results:

$$L_f' = L_f + 0.7\ R_f + 0.7\ L_b$$
$$L_b' = L_b + 0.7\ L_f - 0.7\ R_b$$
$$R_b' = R_b + 0.7\ R_f - 0.7\ L_b$$

To get some feeling for the results from these combinations, consider Fig. 8.7. Here we show the listening situation resulting from an original signal of R_f-only information. Note that the right front speaker is producing R_f as it must according to the equations. The left front speaker and right back speaker are also producing the signal at a lower volume. (An amplitude reduction of 0.7 corresponds to a 3-dB decrease in sound intensity.) However, because the signals from the extra two speakers are equal in intensity, the sound appears to come from between them, exactly along the line to the right front speaker. Therefore, the auditory illusion is created that the original R_f signal is coming from the right front as it should.

Again the question of listening position arises, and here it is much more important than in the discrete method. The listener who moves away from the center of the speaker arrangement will hear the sounds from the nearest speaker more strongly, and the delicate balance of intensity relationships in the equations will be seriously disturbed. Thus, the apparent source of the sound will appear to move. In fact, the listener who sits near the right back speaker will think that essentially all the sound is coming from that speaker.

One commercial attempt to reduce this problem is another electronic means that is called *logic* or *gain-riding* circuitry. This technique involves having amplitude-sensing circuits that constantly monitor the signals for each of the four speakers. If the R_f-only signal were present, then the left front and right back speakers should have signals with amplitudes less than that for the right front speaker (1.0 R_f for right front, 0.7 R_f for the other two). The sensing circuits determine which is strongest and reduce the gain of the others, effectively boosting the already predominate signal. Thus the sound field of the listener who sits near the right back speaker is not so distorted, since the signal from the right front speaker is still much stronger than that from the right back.

The matrixing system, as well as the discrete system, has advantages and disadvantages. The advantages are primarily technical; no new cutter assemblies or new reproducing cartridge designs are needed. Con-

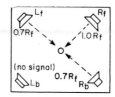

Fig. 8.7. Reproduction of R_f-only original signal using Scheiber equations.

ventional stereo equipment can be used and with matrixing decoders can easily be converted to four-channel operation. ◄──── ✶ ✶ ✶

The disadvantage is that the four original signals are not reproduced as individual signals but only as combinations. It is not possible to remove this constraint; it comes from the fact that two equations cannot be used to solve uniquely for four unknown quantities. ◄──────➤

✶ ✶ ✶

8.3 FOUR-CHANNEL INFORMATION ON FM

Finally, we come to four-channel information transmission via radio waves. The AM radio is not well suited to multichannel broadcasting because of the inherent bandwidth problems discussed in Section 7.4; FM is suited for this type of transmission. In fact, we discuss in Section 7.5.2 how to put two stereo signals plus a third background music signal (SCA) into one FM signal. Several approaches are possible for four-channel broadcasting; however, at this writing the Federal Communications Commission has not decided which approach should be used.

To understand part of the FCC dilemma, let us consider some of the ground rules for FM four-channel operation. (1) We would like the new system to be compatible with existing monophonic receivers; therefore, the main channel must carry $L_f + L_b + R_f + R_b$ information. (2) The new system must be compatible with existing stereo equipment; that is, present equipment with no modification should be able to receive L_f and L_b signals on the left channel and R_f and R_b information on the right channel. (3) The new operation should be compatible, if possible, with existing SCA broadcasting. Recall that the SCA signals are centered on a 67-kHz subcarrier frequency; if the new four-channel methods involve any of the spectrum of 60–75 kHz, all existing SCA equipment must be modified (at rather great expense, considering the amount of equipment involved). (4) The 75-kHz maximum bandwidth must be maintained.

Let us examine two possible approaches to putting four channels on FM. (If you have forgotten the technique of multiplexing, review Section 7.5.2.)

8.3.1 Simple Multiplexing of Each Signal

The simplest approach would be to multiplex each independent signal onto some carrier signal:

0–15	kHz	L_f, main channel
23–53	kHz	R_f, AM modulating 38-kHz carrier
61–91	kHz	L_b, AM modulating 76-kHz carrier
99–129	kHz	R_b, AM modulating 114-kHz carrier
19	kHz	pilot tone for phase and carrier multiples

Such a system is diagrammed in Fig. 8.8. The two advantages to this system are: (1) the four signals are independent with large guard bands

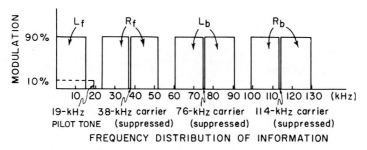

Fig. 8.8. Simple way to put four channels of information onto one FM signal.

separating each frequency region; and (2) a single 19-kHz pilot tone will provide the carrier for each set of sidebands, since 2×19 kHz = 38 kHz, 4×19 kHz = 76 kHz, and 6×19 kHz = 114 kHz. The disadvantage is that it absolutely does not satisfy the FCC ground rules for four-channel transmission. A monophonic receiver will receive only L_f information, existing stereo equipment will sense L_f and R_f but will mix them and destroy the identity of L_f and R_f (L_b and R_b will not be detected at all), and the present SCA band around 67 kHz is covered by the third pair of sidebands. That simple system is clearly rejected.

8.3.2 System Using Phase Shifting

One system, which does satisfy the FCC ground rules, uses the multiplexing technique plus a new phase-shifting trick. The four channels are combined in the following ways:

$$\text{set } 1 = L_f + L_b + R_f + R_b \quad \text{(all information)}$$
$$\text{set } 2 = (L_f + L_b) - (R_f + R_b) \quad \text{(left — right)}$$
$$\text{set } 3 = (L_f + R_f) - (L_b + R_b) \quad \text{(front — back)}$$
$$\text{set } 4 = (L_f + R_b) - (R_f + L_b)$$

The four sets are put into the signal as follows. Set 1, which contains all the acoustic information, is put into the main channel. Thus a monophonic receiver will detect the entire signal information. Set 2, which contains the left (front and back) information minus the right information, is used to amplitude-modulate a 38-kHz carrier. This is exactly the way present stereo information is stored; therefore existing stereo equipment will function properly. Set 3, which contains front minus back information, is used to frequency-modulate another 38-kHz carrier that has been phase-shifted by 90° with respect to the first 38-kHz carrier. (We shall return to phase shifting in a moment.) Set 4 is used to frequency-modulate a 76-kHz carrier but only the upper sideband is transmitted. (This allows the SCA signal space to be undisturbed.) One of the two sidebands is sufficient for information transmission. The system is diagrammed in Fig. 8.9.

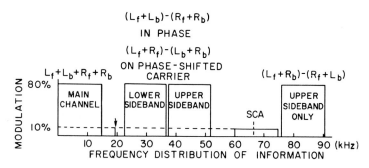

Fig. 8.9.   One proposed scheme for quadraphonic FM transmission.

The phase-shifting trick can be understood if we recall the meaning of phase from Section 6.3. In that discussion we point out that two waves can have exactly the same shape but be shifted from one another in time. That is, at the beginning of a plot of the wave (x equals zero), one wave might have the value zero while the other wave might have a maximum value (see Fig. 8.10. The solid line is a sine wave; the dashed line is a cosine wave.). We say that this second wave is identical to the first wave but shifted in phase by one-quarter wavelength. If we think of a full wavelength as represented by 360°, the quarter wave shift is 90°.

Phase information is meaningless unless we have some unique clock to tell us when to start the measurement. But in the FM signal, we already have such a clock, namely the 19-kHz pilot tone. We can use it as a reference to see whether the 38-kHz signals are inphase, out of phase, or phase-shifted from the 19-kHz pilot tone. The inphase signal contains left minus right information; the signal shifted by 90° contains the front minus back information. Because present stereo receivers only search for the inphase signals, existing equipment is not disturbed by the new information.

Many approaches are possible for incorporating four-channel information into FM. The commercial firms that support the matrixing methods of disc recording are urging the FCC to approve only "matrixed" broadcasting (already in use). The problem of not being able to recover the four independent signals remains, however, and proponents of pure, discrete four-channel operation oppose the approach. The

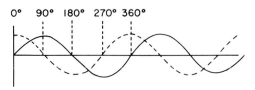

Fig. 8.10.   Two waves shifted by one-quarter wavelength (or 90°).

above discussions are preparatory for a basic understanding of the system to be adopted.

8.4   SUMMARY

(1) To reproduce both the spatial characteristics of an orchestra (or any performing group) and the characteristics of the performance hall, more than two channels of information are required.

(2) Discrete four-channel discs preserve the four independent sets of information. This approach is compatible with existing stereo systems. The new information is stored by frequency-modulating supersonic (30-kHz) carrier frequencies. Disadvantages are mainly technological.

(3) Matrixed four-channel discs do not preserve the four independent sets of information. However, these systems are technologically simple and compatible with existing equipment.

(4) The matrixing approach cannot yield the four original channels independently, since all four sets of information are stored in two grooves. Two equations are not sufficient to solve for four unique unknowns. Discrete discs can recover all four since the two extra sets of 30-kHz, FM-modulated signals provide two new equations (giving four equations for the four unknowns) even though that information is included in the original two grooves.

(5) Logic or gain-riding circuitry can improve the effectiveness of the matrixing approach by reducing the amplitude of the signals sent to the undesired speakers.

(6) No four-channel FM broadcasting approach has been adopted. Multiplexing and phase shifting offer possible solutions. Ground rules of compatibility with existing equipment determine feasibility of various methods.

QUESTIONS

1. What are the advantages of quadraphonic sound reproduction? Disadvantages?
2. Is it possible to have more than four reproducing channels? Would there be any advantages to doing so? Disadvantages?
3. How is it possible to put four sets of information into one record groove? Is it possible to put more than four sets into one groove?
4. In what ways are the coding-decoding methods of discrete four-channel disc recording like conventional FM stereo broadcasting ?
5. Describe how the matrixing method of four-channel recording works. What are its advantages and disadvantages? Why can the four sets of information never be reclaimed in pure form but only in combinations?
6. What is the meaning of phase-shifting? How can it be used to encode different sets of information into the same region of frequency space? How can the information be recovered?

7. Why is the listening position with respect to speaker placement so important in quadraphonic reproduction? Is listening position more important for the discrete method or the matrixing method? Why?

8. How can quadraphonic information be transmitted by radio?

EXERCISES

1. Show that the new right back signal in the original Peter Scheiber matrixing method is actually

$$R_b' = R_b + 0.7R_f - 0.7L_b$$

2. Suppose the input to the Scheiber matrixing system were $R_f = L_f$ only (no R_b or L_b original signal). Figure what each of the four speakers would produce, and draw a sketch of the situation similar to Fig. 8.7. Where would the sound appear to originate to a person sitting exactly in the center of the square speaker arrangement?

3. Suppose the input to the Scheiber matrixing system were L_b only. What would each speaker produce? Where would the sound appear to originate to a person sitting exactly in the center of the square speaker arrangement?

1

INTRODUCTORY MECHANICS

A1.1 LINEAR MOTION WITH CONSTANT ACCELERATION

In these brief paragraphs we try to indicate some of the excitement of the most basic discipline of physics: mechanics. Mechanics, the study of motion, includes both how things move and why they move. We discuss in Chapter 1 why an object will begin to move: some force acts on the object. A force large enough to overcome inertia causes acceleration resulting in motion.

Suppose an object is at rest; that is, the body has initial velocity equal to zero. Then a force F acts on the body. The force could be gravitational, a push, attraction due to charge, or any other force you may think of. Any force will do. What happens to the body? It experiences an acceleration a given by Newton's law:

$$a = \frac{F}{m} \qquad (A1.1)$$

where m is the mass of the body.

Recall that the definition of acceleration is the rate of change of velocity. Thus, if there is an acceleration, the body cannot remain at rest; its velocity v must change. Let us write that quantitatively. Let $\Delta v =$ change in velocity and $t =$ time; then $a = \Delta v/t$, and the change in the velocity is

$$\Delta v = at \qquad (A1.2)$$

Now, Δv means $v - v_i$; the present value of the velocity v minus the initial velocity v_i is the change in the velocity. Therefore, the present value of the velocity is

$$v = v_i + at \qquad (A1.3)$$

Another way to read Eq. (A1.3) is, "The present velocity is equal to the initial velocity plus the change in velocity due to an acceleration."

Note that if $a = 0$ (no force exists), the initial velocity will remain unchanged. If an object is at rest, it will remain at rest until a force causes it to move; if an object is moving, it will continue to move in a straight line until some force acts on it to change its motion. This statement is known as Newton's first law of motion.

Now we know how fast an object will be moving if we know (1) its initial velocity and (2) what acceleration the object is experiencing. What can we say about the position of the object? We can predict the position of a body at any time by knowing one more initial quantity: where the object was initially. For an object moving along a straight line we might indicate its position by x. The initial position would be indicated by x_i. The position of the object at any later time can be written as

$$x = \text{(initial position)} + \begin{pmatrix} \text{distance moved} \\ \text{because of} \\ \text{initial velocity} \end{pmatrix} + \begin{pmatrix} \text{distance moved} \\ \text{because of} \\ \text{acceleration} \end{pmatrix}$$

Let us describe the last two terms one at a time. The distance an object moves because it has velocity is simply

$$\text{distance} = \text{velocity} \times \text{time}$$

the basic "distance = rate $\times$ time" formula taught early in schooling. Thus, the second term in the distance formula is $v_i t$, initial velocity times time.

The last term is more difficult. It involves a *changing* velocity due to acceleration. That term works out to be $(\frac{1}{2})(at^2)$, one-half times the acceleration times the square of the time involved.

Our formula for position, then, is

$$x = x_i + v_i t + (\tfrac{1}{2})at^2 \tag{A1.4}$$

An example may help keep these quantities straight. Suppose an object of mass 2 kg has initial position $x_i = 0$ (we will measure from the initial position), $v_i = 0$ (it is at rest), and the object is acted on by a force of 4 N. Where will the object be and how fast will it be moving at the end of 4 s? To answer these questions, we use Eqs. (A1.3) and (A1.4). However, to use those equations we need the acceleration of the object, so we employ Eq. (A1.1):

$$a = \frac{F}{m} = \frac{4 \text{ N}}{2 \text{ kg}} = \frac{4 \text{ kg·m/s}^2}{2 \text{ kg}} = 2 \text{ m/s}^2$$

Now, we can find the velocity after 4 s:

$$v = v_i + at = 0 + (2 \text{ m/s}^2)(4 \text{ s}) = 8 \text{ m/s}$$

Also, we can find the present position:

$$\begin{aligned} x &= x_i + v_i t + (\tfrac{1}{2})at^2 \\ &= 0 + (0)(4 \text{ s}) + (\tfrac{1}{2})(2 \text{ m/s}^2)(4 \text{ s})^2 \\ &= (\tfrac{1}{2})(2 \text{ m/s}^2)(16 \text{ s}^2) \\ x &= 16 \text{ m} \end{aligned}$$

The object has moved 16 m (about 50 ft) and has a speed of 8 m/s at the end of 4 s.

We have examined only the simplest beginning of the study of motion. Other possibilities include acceleration changing with time and motion not in a straight line—the acceleration changes the direction of the motion as well as the speed. (Quality turntables have an "antiskating" device to compensate for an acceleration of this type. The outer part of the rotating record groove pushes a stylus towards the center of a record. The stylus is accelerated towards the center. The antiskating device compensates for this and applies an outward force to balance and cancel the inward acceleration.)

This elementary discussion is intended to show the power of mechanics: if we know where an object is, how fast it is moving, and what forces are involved, we can predict the motion of the particle at any later time.

A1.2 ENERGY

Let us turn now to energy. Energy exists in many forms: chemical, nuclear, gravitational, solar (which originates from nuclear energy), electrical, magnetic, and mechanical. Here we discuss only the mechanical energy associated with linear motion.

Energy is the ability to do work or to move something. How can an object "do work" on a second object? There are two ways of causing motion. The first way is a moving body colliding with a second body and thereby causing the second body to move. This energy due to motion is called *kinetic* energy from a Greek word meaning "moving." The faster a body moves, the more kinetic energy it has. In fact, the kinetic energy depends on the square of the velocity. A body moving twice as fast as another body of the same mass has four times as much energy as the slower body. It is awesome to realize that an automobile moving at 60 mph has four times as much devastating power as it has at 30 mph. Also, the more mass an object has, the more kinetic energy it will have. The result: the amount of kinetic energy KE in a body is

$$\text{KE} = (\tfrac{1}{2})mv^2 \tag{A1.5}$$

where m is mass and v is velocity.

The second form of mechanical energy is called *potential* energy because the energy is stored in the body. A compressed spring has potential energy. An object hanging in a gravitational field has gravitational potential energy. Someone had to do work to lift the object; that work is stored in the body as potential energy. If the object is released, it will fall (the potential energy will be converted into kinetic energy).

Gravitational potential energy depends on three things: the mass of the object, the acceleration of gravity, and the height of the object. This makes sense, because if we calculate how much work it takes to lift a body to a height h, we have

$$\text{work} = \text{force} \times \text{height} = (ma_g) \times (h) = mgh$$

where the acceleration of gravity a_g is simply written as g. (You may recall astronauts discussing accelerations of 3gs, 4gs, etc.) **On** the surface of the earth, g is about 10 m/s² (9.8 m/s²). All the work done in lifting is stored as potential energy.

One final example may help to show the power of these techniques. Suppose an object of mass 2 kg is 4 m above the ground. If the object is dropped, how fast will it be moving when it hits the ground? First, we calculate the potential energy PE of the object, the work stored in it to lift it to the height of 4 m:

$$PE = mgh = (2 \text{ kg})(10 \text{ m/s}^2)(4 \text{ m}) = 80 \text{ kg·m}^2/\text{s}^2 = 80 \text{ J}$$

This 80 J of potential energy is entirely converted into kinetic energy at the bottom of the fall. (Air friction is small enough to ignore.) So at the bottom of the fall

$$KE = 80 \text{ J} = (\tfrac{1}{2}) mv^2$$

Therefore $v^2 = 2 \times 80 \text{ J}/m = (160 \text{ J})/(2 \text{ kg}) = 80 \text{ m}^2/\text{s}^2$.

$$v = \sqrt{80 \text{ m}^2/\text{s}^2} \cong 9 \text{ m/s}$$

An object dropped from a height of 4 m is moving at 9 m/s (about 30 ft/s) when it hits the ground.

Perhaps it is not obvious that any object, not just a 4-kg mass, dropped from 4 m would have that final speed. We can show this by setting the initial potential energy mgh equal to the final kinetic energy $(\tfrac{1}{2}) mv^2$ and solving for the velocity v. That is,

$$mgh = (\tfrac{1}{2}) mv^2$$
$$v = \sqrt{2gh} \tag{A1.6}$$

The mass cancels out; the final velocity of *any* object when dropped depends only on the height and the acceleration of gravity (ignoring air resistance)! The same formulas may be used to calculate the height an object was dropped from if we know the final speed of the object.

If we wish to put a man on the moon, we can calculate the necessary trajectory by energy techniques. If we want to design a tone arm for a turntable, we can do so with other energy techniques. The concept of energy is broad and general.

APPENDIX **2**

CONSUMER CONSIDERATIONS

The material in this book is designed to help prepare consumers as well as beginning students of science. There is no easy answer to the question, "How do I buy a stereo?" A sound system should be suited for particular needs. Many articles are available to assist in assessing one's needs. Back issues of the periodicals given in the reading list contain helpful articles, such as "How Much Power Do I Need?", "How to choose a Turntable," "Stereo or Four-Channel?", etc. Decide your needs before comparing equipment.

Having determined your needs, you are next faced with the question, "What equipment do I buy?" We cannot answer that question either, but we can help you compare equipment. It is difficult to determine that equipment is very good, but it is not too difficult to determine that it is very bad.

In this section we survey the specifications used to rate various pieces of high fidelity equipment. We present what we regard as minimum specifications that may be used to compare products from various manufacturers.

Remember that these are minimum specifications. Clearly some available equipment will have characteristics significantly better than those given here. To have such excellent equipment is fine except when devices of significantly differing characteristics are combined in one system. (A chain is only as strong as its weakest link.) For example, a super–high power amplifier with immeasurably low noise characteristics will amplify all the noise from the preamplifier. Thus, one noisy component can dominate the behavior of an entire system.

In addition, we must be aware that the transducer elements of a system usually provide the greatest contribution to the total distortion. Electromechanical devices are difficult to make, as we discuss in the text; the perfect transducer is yet to come. Of the transducers, loudspeakers are the biggest offenders. Different loudspeakers clearly sound different. Prospective buyers should always make an effort to listen to various loudspeakers under comparative tests, side by side in the same room. No matter how much one reads about a speaker a buyer will not know how it sounds until listening to it personally.

159

Even after selecting a speaker system that sounds great in a store, one may find that the same speakers sound not so great in the living room at home, since the room itself significantly affects the response. (Some experts recommend that a buyer arrange for a home trial period. Most dealers are willing.) A small change in the location of a speaker from high on a shelf to the floor may produce a dramatic change in sound. (It is the author's opinion that buying loudspeakers is the single, most critical step in the purchase of a high fidelity system.) The more time, care, and listening spent in this step, the more enjoyment for many years to come.

The following list of specifications has been compiled mainly from reading. A similar list has been published in *Insights into Modern Communications: From Hifi Sound to Laser Beams* (see the reading list). For certain specifications, some experts may recommend more stringent minimum requirements. This list will, however, identify inferior specifications. In each case where we give a number, we identify whether the number should be larger or smaller for improved characteristics. CAUTION! A frequency range of 20–20,000 Hz means nothing without also knowing frequency response; that is, 20–20,000 Hz ± 1 dB is excellent whereas 20–20,000 Hz ± 15 dB is abysmal. In all these specifications, frequency range and response must be read together. Beware of the manufacturer who says 20–20,000 Hz without mentioning response.

A. Amplifiers
1. Frequency range: 20–20,000 Hz (or greater).
2. Response: ±1 dB (or less) over entire range.
3. Total harmonic distortion (THD): 1% (or less) when amplifier is driven to full power.
4. Intermodulation distortion (IM): 1% (or less) when amplifier is driven to full power.
5. Power: No definable minimum to power ratings exists. The power you need depends on speaker choice, room size, whether you plan to add other speakers later, etc. Decide your power needs before you start.

In comparing power ratings of various amplifiers, compare only *continuous* power ratings with all channels simultaneously driven. Continuous power (sometimes called RMS [root-mean-square] power, the technique of averaging sine waves) is the maximum continuous power the amplifier can produce without exceeding its distortion ratings. Be sure to notice whether the specification is power per channel or total power for all channels. Furthermore, compare output power for the same load: that is, an amplifier may produce 30 W into a 4-Ω load but only 15 W into an 8-Ω load. Be sure you compare ratings for the same load.

Do not attempt to use "music power" or "peak power" ratings. These numbers may be inflated to give a false impression of a weak amplifier.

6. Signal-to-noise (S/N) ratio: 60 dB (or greater). This number is the ratio of the output of the amplifier under conditions of desired signal (full output) and no input signal (all that is heard is hum or noise). The larger the ratio, the smaller the noise.

7. Phono input sensitivity: Voltage needed to drive the amplifier to full rated output. No defined minimum exists, but the phono cartridge to be selected should match this specification.

8. Maximum phono input voltage: Input voltage that will cause obvious distortion in the amplifier. Normally this number should be 10 (or greater) times larger than the phono input sensitivity.

9. Damping factor: 4 (or greater). See text for discussion.

B. Phono Cartridge

1. Frequency range:
   (a) Stereo: 20–20,000 Hz (or greater).
   (b) Quadraphonic: 20–50,000 Hz (or greater).

2. Frequency response: ± 3 dB (or smaller) over entire frequency range.

3. Compliance: 10×10^{-6} cm/dyne (or greater). This number refers to the freedom of the stylus to respond to forces from the groove wall of a record. A large number means that the stylus is very free to move and records will not wear out as quickly.

4. Tracking force: ¾ g to 2.5 g. (The tracking force is the effective weight needed to keep the stylus tip in the record groove under tracking conditions expected on records.) The smaller the number, the longer the life of the records as well as the stylus tip. (Note that the industry uses "grams" to specify force. "Two-gram force" means that force caused by the weight of a 2-g mass.)

5. Stereo separation: 20 dB (or greater). See text for discussion (Section 5.1.3).

6. Stylus tip: Diamond for normal use; sapphire for short-term use only.

C. Tone Arm

1. Tracking error: 3° (or less). This number refers to the maximum angular difference between the angle of the tone arm and the angle of the cutter used to produce a record. Ideally, the reproducing tone arm should have the same configuration as the cutter. If the angular difference is larger, the voltage output of the cartridge will be reduced.

2. Resonant frequency: 10 Hz (or less). At this frequency of vibration the tone arm itself will vibrate in resonance with a driving frequency from the record groove or a loudspeaker. To prevent tone arm vibration this frequency should be significantly less than the lowest frequency on any record to be played.

D. Turntables
   1. Speed accuracy: 1% (or less). Speed accuracy is a comparison of
       the average rotational speed of the table to any desired speed such
       as 33⅓ rpm. An error of 1% is large enough to cause noticeable
       differences in musical pitch from references such as a piano, etc.,
       but not large enough to cause objectionable pitch differences
       for music played without reference comparison. Some turntables
       offer adjustable speed controls.
   2. Wow and flutter: 0.2% (or less). These numbers refer to varia-
       tions in turntable speed while it is playing. These variations
       are much more objectionable than simple speed error, since
       the variable speed causes musical pitch to change as one listens.
       Slow, periodic variations are called wow; more rapid variations
       (like vibrations in the human voice) are called flutter. Both
       should be minimized.
   3. Rumble: −35 dB (or better, where −50 dB is better than −35
       dB). Rumble is mechanical vibration of the turntable drive sys-
       tem that causes vibration of the stylus and therefore causes its
       own output from the cartridge; −35 dB means the signal gen-
       erated because of rumble should be at least 35 dB lower than the
       desired signals produced from proper tracking of the record
       groove.
E. FM Tuners
   1. Audio frequency range: 30–15,000 Hz (or greater).
   2. Audio frequency response: ±1 dB (or smaller).
   3. Sensitivity: 3 μV (or smaller) for 30-dB quieting (1 μV = 10^{-6} V).
       This specification gives the amplitude of the input voltage signal
       necessary for the tuner to produce an output signal at least 30
       dB greater than the noise level. The smaller the sensitivity (for
       30-dB quieting), the better distant signals can be received. Be-
       cause the strength of the input signal depends on the quality of
       the antenna used, a tuner with a poor (large) sensitivity may
       still receive distant signals with an elaborate antenna system.
   4. Signal-to-noise ratio (S/N): 60 dB or greater at full output.
   5. Total harmonic distortion (THD): 1% (or less) at full output.
   6. Intermodulation distortion (IM): 1% (or less) at full output.
   7. Selectivity: 60 dB (or greater). This number refers to the ability
       of the tuner to separate two adjacent signals on the FM band;
       that is, to accept one and reject the other. In metropolitan areas
       with many stations, this specification can be quite important.
   8. Capture ratio: 3 dB (or smaller). Capture ratio is a measure of
       a tuner's ability to separate two (or more) stations on the same
       channel. The separation is done by "phase-locking" the tuner
       on the phase of one of the signals (the stronger one). Since it is
       very unlikely that any two signals will have the same phase, one
       signal may be rejected. The 3 dB corresponds to difference in

signal strength necessary for the tuner capture circuitry to recognize one of the signals as stronger. This specification is important to tuners located between two metropolitan areas that may have stations on the same channel.

F. Tape Deck

A tape deck is a tape machine that does not contain an amplifier and must be used as an input unit to an existing audio system. If the tape machine has an amplifier, the unit is commonly called a tape recorder. The amplifier section, if any, should be judged according to the specifications listed above for amplifiers.

1. Frequency range:
   (a) **Open reel decks:** 30–18,000 Hz (or larger) at $7\frac{1}{2}$ in/s or 19 cm/s.
   (b) **Cassette decks:** 30–15,000 Hz (or larger) at $1\frac{7}{8}$ in/s or 4.76 cm/s.
2. Frequency response: ± 3 dB or (smaller) over entire frequency range.
3. Signal-to-noise:
   (a) **Without Dolby noise reduction:** 50 dB (or higher).
   (b) **With Dolby noise reduction:** 55 dB (or higher).
4. Stereo separation: 30 dB (or higher).
5. Speed accuracy: 1% (or smaller). See turntable discussion.
6. Wow and flutter: 0.2% (or less). See turntable discussion.

Good luck!

GLOSSARY

ABSOLUTE ZERO: The temperature at which all available energy has been removed from an object.

ACCELERATION: The rate of change of velocity.

ACCEPTOR IMPURITY: An impurity atom having fewer bonding electrons than the atoms of the host crystal. When added to a semiconductor crystal, it creates a hole state, making p-type material.

ALTERNATING CURRENT (AC): A flow of electric charge that periodically reverses its direction. The charge builds to a maximum flow in one direction, decreases to zero, then builds to a maximum in the other direction, etc.

AMPERE: The unit of electric current equivalent to one coulomb of charge per second.

AMPLIFIER: A device that increases the power of a signal by allowing the input signal to control the magnitude of the output signal.

AMPLITUDE: The maximum deviation represented by a wave motion. For example, as a hanging spring oscillates up and down, amplitude is the maximum displacement of the spring from the rest position.

AMPLITUDE-MODULATED: A method of putting information onto a wave by changing the amplitude of the wave.

ANODE: The positive terminal of a device, such as the plate in a vacuum tube.

ANTINODES: The positions of maximum deviation in standing waves.

ATOM: The smallest building block of a chemical element having the properties of the element. An atom is an electrically neutral combination of electrons, protons, and neutrons.

ATMOSPHERIC PRESSURE: Force per unit area due to molecules of air colliding with an object when the air is undisturbed. Sound waves cause the pressure at a point to rise above and fall below atmospheric pressure.

BAFFLE: A partition used to increase the length of travel of sound waves; used in loudspeaker enclosures to increase bass response.

BASE: The region of a bipolar transistor that receives the charge carriers injected from the emitter. This element corresponds in function to the control grid of a vacuum tube.

BASS: Low frequencies; loosely defined to be frequencies below 250 Hz.

BATTERY: A source of DC voltage; usually a chemical cell, but could be solar, nuclear, or thermal.

BINARY NUMBERS: A system of numbers consisting of combinations of two digits, 0 and 1. This system can be conveniently represented electronically by OFF-ON states of switches.

BIPOLAR TRANSISTOR: A semiconductor device having two np junctions resulting from a sandwich structure of three semiconducting layers called emitter, base, and collector.

CAPACITANCE: The property of a system or device that allows it to store charge (when a voltage is applied to it) by means of an electric field; measured in farads (F) defined as 1 coulomb per volt.

CAPACITOR: A device consisting primarily of two conducting sheets separated by an insulating layer; can store charge, block direct current, and pass alternating current to a degree depending on the capacitance and the frequency.

CARDIOID RESPONSE: A microphone response pattern shaped somewhat like a heart.

CARRIER WAVE: A wave of constant amplitude and frequency that may be modulated to carry information.

CATHODE: The negative terminal of a device, such as the filament or electron source in a vacuum tube.

CHANNEL: A single path for storing or transmitting signals, such as the left and right channels in a stereo system.

CHARGE: The property of nature that creates electric fields. The elements of charge are the electron (negative) and the proton (positive). Unit of charge is the coulomb (C), which is equal to the charge of 6×10^{18} protons.

CHIP: A small device that contains solid-state circuits, connecting terminals, and protective cover.

CLIPPING: The form of distortion that arises when an amplifier cannot put out sufficient power. Instead of smooth output waveforms, the waves show flat tops.

COLLECTOR: The part of a transistor through which most charge carriers leave the transistor. The collector is analogous to the plate in a vacuum tube.

COMPLEX NUMBER: A number having both real and imaginary (mathematical terms) parts; a number having both magnitude and phase.

COMPLIANCE: The ability of a mechanical system to yield or move in response to a force; the inverse of the spring constant.

CONDUCTION OF ELECTRICITY: The flow of charge. Normally electrons are conducted through metals. In liquids and semiconductors both positive and negative charge may flow.

CONDUCTION OF HEAT: The transmission of thermal energy by the mechanical collisions of atoms and molecules.

CONDUCTOR: A material through which electricity flows easily. Metals are good conductors.

CONE: The part of a loudspeaker that moves in and out (also called the diaphragm); usually made of reinforced paper or impregnated cloth.

CONVECTION: The transmission of thermal energy due to the lower density of warm air (or other fluid). The higher density cold air pushes the warm air upwards.

COULOMB: The unit of charge, abbreviated C. (*See* CHARGE.)

CROSS TALK: The presence of a signal in one channel of a system coming from a signal in another channel.

CRYSTAL: An object having its atoms arranged in a periodic lattice structure, often having interesting physical properties. Diamond is a crystal of carbon.

CURRENT: A flow of charge. In conventional literature current is defined to be the flow of positive charge. In this book, electron flow is discussed more often than current, since electrons are the charge carriers in most situations. In ambiguous cases, "electron flow" is the term used. "Current" and "electron flow" are used interchangeably if there is no ambiguity of the direction of electron flow. Unit: ampere (A), equal to a flow of one coulomb per second.

DAMPING: 1. Friction applied to a system to reduce its tendency to oscillate for long times. 2. Resistance applied to an electrical circuit to reduce its tendency to oscillate.

DECIBEL: The unit used for measuring the relative intensity levels of sounds.

DENSITY: The mass per unit volume (kg/m^3) of a material. The density of water is 1000 kg/m^3. Materials with lesser density float on water, those with greater density sink.

DIAPHRAGM: The part of a microphone, loudspeaker, or earphone that moves in response to a signal (also called the "cone" in a loudspeaker).

DIFFUSION: The motion of charge across a *pn* junction due to thermal energy.

DIGITAL STORAGE: The storage of a signal by numbers describing the amplitude of the signal for various values of time. Its advantage is that little or no noise is introduced into the stored signal.

DIODE: A two-element electronic device (either tube or solid state) that permits electrons to flow through it in one direction but not the other.

DIRECT CURRENT: A one-directional flow of current. Magnitude of current (or voltage) may change, but not direction (polarity).

DISCRETE RECORDING: A method of recording in which each signal is preserved as a separate channel.

DISPLACEMENT: The distance a system has moved away from its equilibrium or rest position.

DISTORTION: Any change in a signal as it is being processed or transmitted.

DOLBY TECHNIQUE: A method for reducing tape noise or hiss that involves boosting selected signals during recording and reducing them on playback.

DOMAIN SIZE: The size of small magnetic particles embedded in the surface layer of recording tape.

DONOR: An impurity atom having more bonding electrons than the atoms of the host crystal lattice. It donates electrons to the crystal producing n-type material.

DOPANT: An impurity put into a semiconducting crystal to produce n- or p-type material.

DRAIN: The element of a field-effect transistor that corresponds to the plate of a vacuum tube.

DRIFT: The motion of charge across a pn junction due to the electric field set up in the space charge region.

DYNAMIC TRANSDUCER: A transducer that has a moving coil. (Not a rigid definition; sometimes moving magnet transducers are referred to as dynamic.)

ELECTRICAL IMPEDANCE: Loosely defined, the effective resistance of a circuit to an alternating voltage. Precisely defined, the complex number ratio of voltage to current in an AC system. Unit: ohm (Ω).

ELECTRIC FIELD: A field set up in space due to the presence of charge. Field lines are drawn from positive to negative charges and point in the direction of the force a positive charge would experience.

ELECTRON: The smallest unit of negative charge that cannot be divided. Possesses a magnetic field due to intrinsic spin.

ELECTROSTATIC: Term that describes the effects of charges at rest (as compared with flowing charges).

EMITTER: The part of a transistor corresponding to the filament or cathode of a vacuum tube; injects charge carriers into the base region.

ENERGY: The ability to do work.

ENERGY GAP: A forbidden region in the spectrum of energy states for electrons in a material. The width of the gap determines whether a material is a metal, a semiconductor, or an insulator.

EQUILIBRIUM POSITION: The natural, at-rest position for a system.

EXPONENTIAL HORN: A coupling device attached to a loudspeaker to increase the energy transfer efficiency to the air. Its shape is described by an exponential equation.

FERMI LEVEL: The highest energy level of electrons in a material at temperature of absolute zero.

FIELD-EFFECT TRANSISTOR: A solid-state device (similar in operation to a vacuum tube) that uses an electric field to control the flow of charge. Elements are called source, gate, and drain.

FILAMENT: The heated element in a vacuum tube that emits electrons (or heats a cathode causing it to emit electrons).

FLETCHER-MUNSON CURVES: Plots relating the response of the human ear to the intensity and frequency of sound.

FORCE: The cause of acceleration of a particle.

FORWARD BIASED: A wiring configuration in which a diode or *pn* junction conducts well.

FREQUENCY: The number of oscillations per unit time.

FREQUENCY MODULATION: A method of alternatively increasing and decreasing the carrier frequency. The number of times per second the frequency is changed back and forth (a complete cycle) is the frequency of the signal, and the amount of deviation from the original carrier frequency gives the amplitude of the signal.

FRICTION: The force between materials in contact.

GAP: 1. The separation between the pole pieces of a magnet or of a tape-recording or reproducing head. 2. *See* ENERGY GAP.

GAS: The state of matter characterized by very weak interatomic forces. Air is a gas composed primarily of nitrogen and oxygen gases.

GATE: A wire mesh element in a vacuum tube that creates an electric field to control the flow of electrons across the tube.

HARMONIC DISTORTION: The distortion characterized by the creation of harmonic frequencies $2f$, $3f$, $4f$, etc., of a given input frequency f.

HOLES: Vacant allowed energy states in a material. Holes propagate through a material as though they were positive charges with the mass of an electron.

HOOKE'S LAW: An equation relating the restoring force of a spring to its stretch.

HYSTERESIS: The amount of lag between the magnetization inside a material and an applied magnetic field.

INDUCTANCE: The property of an electrical circuit that opposes any change in the current in the circuit. This opposition arises from the energy stored in the magnetic field created by the current.

INDUCTION: The creation of voltage across a conductor by a magnetic field. Induction may be caused by the motion of the conductor in a magnetic field or by changing the magnetic field intensity in the presence of a conductor.

INDUCTOR: Usually a conductor formed into a coil; exhibits inductance.

INPUT: The signal used to drive a system; signal could be electrical, mechanical, acoustical, etc.

INSULATOR: A material having a very high resistance to the flow of electric current. The spectrum of allowed energies of the elecrons in the material has a wide gap at the Fermi level.

INTEGRATED CIRCUIT: A combination of solid-state electronic elements attached together as one unit.

INTENSITY: A quantity used to express the strength of a signal. In a sound wave, intensity equals the power per unit area being transmitted by the wave.

INTENSITY LEVEL: The relative comparison of the intensities of sounds; expressed in decibels, compared to the zero dB reference of 10^{-12} watts per meter squared.

INTERMODULATION DISTORTION: The creation of new frequency components to a signal originally composed of two frequency components, f_1 and f_2. The new signals may be sums or differences of integral multiples of the original components, such as $2f_1 + 3f_2$ or $2f_1 - f_2$.

JOULE: The unit of energy or work equal to one newton-meter. A joule (J) is roughly the amount of work necessary to lift an apple from the floor to a table top.

KILOGRAM: The commonly used unit of mass; roughly equivalent to 2.2 lb.

KINETIC ENERGY: The energy an object has due to its motion. Measured in joules, it is equal to one-half the mass times the velocity squared.

LINEAR: A term describing the response of a system to a driving force in which the output is directly proportional to the input. For example, doubling the input signal produces a doubling of the output signal.

LOAD: A device that absorbs power; often a transducer such as a loudspeaker.

LONGITUDINAL WAVE: A wave in which the displacements of the medium are in the direction the wave is traveling.

LOUDSPEAKER: A transducer that converts electrical signals into sound.

MAGNETIC: 1. A substance that becomes magnetized in the presence of a magnetic field. 2. An atom that produces a magnetic field.

MAGNETIC FIELD: 1. The disturbance in space that results from the flow of electric charge. All magnetic fields are created by current.

2. The disturbance in space that results from the presence of magnetic material—material containing atoms that are magnetic because
of electron current.

MAGNETIC OXIDE: The material, in the form of small particles embedded in an elastic binder, used in the coating on recording tape.
The name comes from the chemical combination of a magnetic
atom such as iron (Fe) or chromium (Cr) with oxygen.

MASS: 1. The amount of material in a body. 2. The resistance (often
called inertia) of a body to changes in velocity. Measured in kilo-
grams.

MATRIXED RECORDING: A method for recording several sets of information into fewer channels. Presently used by some manufacturers to put four signals into two channels. On playback the original sets of information cannot be independently restored, but convenient combinations of signals may be regained.

MECHANICAL IMPEDANCE: The ratio of the driving force to the
velocity of a mechanical system. Because the force and velocity are
not always inphase, mechanical impedance is a complex (having real
and imaginary parts) quantity.

MECHANICS: The discipline of physics dealing with motion and
forces.

METAL: A material in which the spectrum of allowed electron energies
is continuous at the Fermi level. These materials are usually good
conductors of both electricity and heat.

MICROPHONE: A transducer that converts acoustic energy into electrical energy.

MIDRANGE FREQUENCIES: Loosely defined to be those frequencies
in the range of 250–3500 Hz.

MODULATION: The process of using one signal to change or control
another.

MOLECULE: The smallest unit of a chemical compound showing the
properties of the compound; composed of two or more atoms.

MONOPHONIC: A system having only one channel of information.

MOSFET: A Metal-Oxide-Semiconductor Field-Effect Transistor; that
is, a field-effect transistor whose active elements are composed of
a metal, an oxide compound, and a semiconducting material.

MULTICHANNEL STORAGE: A method for simultaneously storing
more than one channel of information.

NEWTON: The unit for force; equal to one kilogram-meter per second
per second; abbreviated N.

NEWTON'S LAWS: Laws of motion discovered by Sir Isaac Newton.
The laws form the basis of the discipline of mechanics and completely describe the motion of particles.

NODES: The points on a standing wave where the displacement is always zero.

NONLINEAR RESPONSE: Response of a system to a driving force or signal, in which the output is not directly proportional to the input. For example, doubling the input signal does not result in an exact doubling of the output signal.

n-TYPE MATERIAL: Semiconducting material that has been doped with impurity atoms having more bonding electrons than do the atoms of the host material; a semiconducting material whose primary charge carriers are electrons.

OHM: The basic unit of electrical resistance and impedance. The ohm (Ω) is equal to one volt per ampere.

OHM'S LAW: The basic relation of voltage, current, and resistance, $V = IR$; i.e., the current flowing through a body is directly proportional to the voltage supplied and inversely proportional to the resistance of the body.

OSCILLATION: One complete cycle of motion of a system demonstrating cyclic behavior.

OUTPUT: The signal produced by a system; could be electrical, mechanical, acoustical, etc.

PARALLEL WIRING: A configuration of electrical connections in which elements are connected to the same terminals and electron flow can branch out over two or more paths.

PERIOD: The amount of time for one oscillation of a system; equal to the inverse of frequency. Symbol: T.

PHASE: A relative measure of progress in simple harmonic motion or a relative comparison of two different waves. For example, if one wave is described as having positive maximum displacement at the same instant another wave has negative maximum, the two are said to be out of phase—differing in phase by one-half cycle.

PHOTOCELL: A device whose electrical properties are changed by the presence of light and whose output current depends on incident light.

PHOTON: The fundamental unit of electromagnetic radiation. The photon has an energy equal to Planck's constant h times the frequency f of the radiation.

PIEZOELECTRIC CRYSTAL: A crystalline material that develops a spontaneous voltage difference between its sides when bent or distorted in shape.

PILOT TONE: A single frequency signal added to stereo FM broadcasts for transmitting phase and frequency reference information.

PLANCK'S CONSTANT: A fundamental constant of nature. In this book Planck's constant (h) occurs in the expression for the energy of a photon.

PLATE: The positive element (anode) of a vacuum tube.

POLE PIECE: One end of a magnet; usually one side of a pair of pole pieces that are separated by a gap.

PORTED ENCLOSURE: A loudspeaker enclosure that has an opening in one wall. Also called a vented enclosure.

POTENTIAL: The energy per unit charge (volt, V) in an electric field.

POTENTIAL ENERGY: The energy (joule, J) an object has when acted on by a field.

POTENTIOMETER: A variable resistance used to control voltage.

POWER: The rate at which energy is supplied or expended. The unit of power is the watt (W), equal to one joule per second.

PREAMPLIFIER: An amplifier designed to boost very weak signals to acceptable levels for further amplification. Preamplifiers contain circuitry that corrects for altered frequency response such as the recording characteristic used for disc and tape recording.

PRESSURE: The force per unit area applied to an object by the molecules in a medium such as air.

PROTON: The smallest unit of positive charge (equal in magnitude to the charge of an electron). The proton has a mass 1836 times greater than the electron and exists in the nucleus of the atom.

p-TYPE MATERIAL: Semiconducting material that has been doped with impurity atoms having fewer bonding electrons than do the atoms of the host; a semiconducting material whose primary charge carriers are holes.

QUADRAPHONIC: A system having four separate channels of audio information.

RADIATION COOLING: Loss of heat by the emission of electromagnetic waves such as light or infrared.

RADIO: A method of transmitting information via electromagnetic waves.

RECORDING CHARACTERISTIC: Intentional altering of the amplitude versus frequency relation for recorded sound for the purpose of maximizing the storage capability of a recording medium. Must be compensated for on playback.

RESISTANCE: The property of a body that determines the magnitude of the current flowing through it for a given applied voltage. Unit: ohm, Ω.

RESISTOR: A device used in electrical circuits to provide certain amounts of resistance.

RESONANCE: The condition that results when a body or an electrical circuit is caused to oscillate at its natural frequency. The resulting motion is inphase with the driving force and develops very large amplitude.

RETENTIVITY: The capacity of retaining magnetization after an external magnetic field is removed from an object.

REVERSE BIASED: The wiring arrangement of a diode or a *pn* junction of a semiconductor for which the diode or junction is not conducting.

RIBBON MICROPHONE: A type of microphone in which the moving element is a small ribbon of conducting material.

SEMICONDUCTOR: A material in which the spectrum of allowed electron energies has a small gap at the Fermi level. These materials form the basis of solid-state electronics.

SERIES WIRING: A method of connecting components in an electrical circuit end-to-end allowing only a single path for the flow of current.

SIDEBAND: A band of radio frequencies on each side of the carrier frequency, produced by modulation (both AM and FM).

SIGNAL: Information transmitted via some medium.

SIMPLE HARMONIC MOTION: Periodic motion whose force is characterized by Hooke's law.

SINE WAVE: A form of oscillatory wave motion resulting from simple harmonic motion.

SOLID STATE: The state of matter characterized by strong binding forces and rigid shape.

SOLID-STATE DEVICE: An electronic device composed of semiconductor elements rather than vacuum tubes.

SOUND: Vibrational mechanical energy being transmitted through a medium.

SOURCE: The part of a field-effect transistor that ejects the charge carriers into the channel. Similar to the cathode or filament in a vacuum tube.

SPACE CHARGE REGION: The region, surrounding a *pn* junction, charged by the diffusion of charge carriers.

SPRING CONSTANT: The characteristic of a physical system that determines the magnitude of the restoring force when the system is deformed; *see* HOOKE'S LAW.

STANDING WAVES: The wave motion that results from two oppositely directed waves of the same frequency traveling in the same medium; characterized by stationary nodal points.

STEREOPHONIC: Three-dimensional sound; that is, sound in which spatial extent is evident. Stereophonic sound is produced by recording with two microphones located at different positions and playing back with two differently placed loudspeakers. Two channels of information are necessary.

SUSPENSION: The part of a loudspeaker of a microphone that attaches the diaphragm to the frame; flexible and provides a restoring force to the diaphragm when stretched.

TAPE: A ribbon of plastic coated with a magnetic powder used in recording.

TEMPERATURE: A measure of the average kinetic energy of the particles in a body, expressed in Kelvins (K), degrees Celsius (° C), or degrees Farenheit (° F).

THERMAL ENERGY: The energy, commonly referred to as heat, due to the motions of particles in a body; measured in joules (J).

TONE ARM: The part of a turntable that carries the reproducing cartridge or transducer.

TRANSDUCER: A device that converts energy from one form into another; for example, a loudspeaker is an electroacoustic transducer.

TRANSISTOR: A solid-state electronics device composed of three or more elements, usually in a sandwich arrangement. The emitter, base, and collector correspond roughly to the filament, grid, and plate of a vacuum tube. The transistor can be used as an amplifier.

TRANSVERSE WAVE: A wave in which the displacements of the medium are perpendicular to the direction the wave is traveling.

TREBLE: The part of the audio frequency spectrum corresponding to high frequencies.

TRIODE: A three-element vacuum tube used most often as an amplifier; composed of a negative filament or cathode that emits electrons, a grid, and a positive plate.

TURNTABLE: A device used for rotating discs at certain speeds for playback.

TWEETER: Loudspeakers designed to reproduce very high frequency signals.

VACANCY STATE: An unfilled electron energy state; *see* HOLE.

VACUUM TUBE: An electronic device consisting of elements sealed in a vacuum; usually has a heated filament or cathode as a source of electrons (photocell is exception).

VELOCITY: The speed of an object or the rate at which the position is changing.

VOICE COIL: The part of a microphone or loudspeaker that moves in the gap of a magnet; attached to the diaphragm.

VOLTAGE: The difference of potential between two points in a circuit. *See* POTENTIAL.

VOLUME: 1. The amount of space occupied. 2. The psychological response called loudness.

WATT: The unit of power, equal to one joule per second. Abbreviated: W.

WAVE: A disturbance that propagates through a medium by periodically displacing the particles of the medium (mechanical waves) or a disturbance of an electric or magnetic field that propagates through space.

WAVELENGTH: The distance between adjacent similar points on a wave.

WAVE RELATION: The basic relation of frequency and wavelength to the velocity of travel of a wave.

WOOFER: A loudspeaker designed to reproduce very low frequency sounds.

WORK: The product of the force applied times the distance an object moves under the influence of that force. Unit: joule (J).

MATERIALS FOR FURTHER READING

The following list of materials is intended to encourage further study of the topics covered in this book. Both technical and nontechnical sources are included, arranged by subject matter. It is impossible for such a list to be complete, but these materials will serve as a starting point for further study.

With one exception, periodicals are not included in the reading list because of the great volume of material contained therein. The following periodicals will, however, be very useful to anyone interested in sound reproduction:

Popular, less technical (more emphasis on music and performance, less on electronics): *Stereo Review; High Fidelity.*

Popular, more technical: *Audio; Absolute Sound; Popular Electronics.*

Technical: *Journal of the Acoustical Society of America; Journal of the Audio Engineering Society.*

In addition, interesting articles on sound and the physics of music may be found in back issues of *Scientific American* and *Physics Today.*

BASIC PHYSICS
Faugh, Jerry S., and Kuhn, Karl F. 1976. *Physics for People Who Think They Don't Like Physics.* Saunders, Philadelphia. As the title suggests, this book is intended to appeal to a broad spectrum of people with little or no background in science. The use of cartoons adds to its appeal.

Hewitt, Paul G. 1974. *Conceptual Physics,* 2d ed. Little, Brown, Boston. This book, which nearly everyone can read and enjoy without instructor assistance, is an excellent nonmathematical treatment of basic physics.

MORE ADVANCED PHYSICS
Smith, Alpheus W., and Cooper, John N. 1972. *Elements of Physics,* 8th ed. McGraw-Hill, New York. An established text for persons with a working knowledge of algebra and trigonometry, this book contains a good section on sound.

Weidner, Richard T., and Sells, Robert L. 1975. *Elementary Physics: Classical and Modern*. Allyn, Bacon, Boston. For persons with a rudimentary knowledge of calculus, this text offers a good treatment of simple harmonic motion and wave behavior.

SOUND AND THE PHYSICS OF MUSIC
Backus, John. 1969. *The Acoustical Foundations of Music*. Norton, New York. A standard text for many courses on the physics of music, this book offers an easy-to-read, nonmathematical approach to the study of sound. It is highly recommended.
Benade, Arthur H. 1960. *Horns, Strings, and Harmony*. Anchor Books (Doubleday), Garden City, N.Y. Long a favorite for lay readers, this book still offers an excellent introduction to sound. Highly recommended for high school students.
———. 1976. *Fundamentals of Musical Acoustics*. Oxford Univ. Press, New York. An excellent book with strong emphasis on music, written by a skilled physicist with considerable research experience on musical instruments.
Culver, Charles A. 1956. *Musical Acoustics*, 4th ed. McGraw-Hill, New York.
Denes, Peter B., and Pinson, Elliot N. 1963. *The Speech Chain*. Bell Telephone Lab., Murray Hill, N.J. Though somewhat dated now, this book still offers an excellent introduction to the mechanisms of hearing and speech.
Josephs, Jess J. 1967. *The Physics of Musical Sound*. Van Nostrand, Princeton, N.J.
Van Bergeijk, William A.; Pierce, John R.; and David, Edward E., Jr. 1960. *Waves and the Ear*. Anchor Books (Doubleday), Garden City, N.Y. Highly recommended for persons with little science background.

SOUND REPRODUCTION

General
Adams, Arthur R.; Harper, Ralph; Johnson, Kenneth W.; and Walker, Willard. 1975. *Insights into Modern Communications: From Hi-Fi Sound to Laser Beams*. Burgess, Minneapolis. This student laboratory guide was constructed for an introductory physics course at Southern Illinois University, Carbondale. It contains a useful treatment of how to read manufacturer's specifications for sound equipment.
Bernstein, J. L. 1966. *Audio Systems*. Wiley, New York.
Boyce, W. F. 1973. *Hifi Stereo Handbook*. Sams, Indianapolis. This is one of a series of books from this publisher that treats some aspect of the consumer's use of electronic equipment. These books are

usually interesting, well illustrated, and appropriate for an amateur audience.

Davis, Don, and Davis, Carolyn. 1975. *Sound System Engineering.* Sams, Indianapolis. An excellent resource book for persons responsible for public address systems.

Fantel, H. 1973. *ABC's of Hifi and Stereo,* 2d ed. Sams, Indianapolis.

Feldman, Leonard. 1973. *Four Channel Sound.* Sams, Indianapolis. Contains technological know-how necessary for maximum capability; addresses both techniques and limitations of four-channel systems.

Jones, E. H. 1961. *Audio Frequency Engineering.* Chatto and Windus, London. Although dated, this book still offers a useful, high level introduction to engineering aspects of audio.

Olson, Harry F. 1972. *Modern Sound Reproduction.* Van Nostrand Reinhold, New York. Not for the beginner, this volume is an advanced reference work of high quality.

Rosenthal, M. P. 1969. *How to Select and Use Hifi and Stereo Equipment,* 2 vols. Hayden, New York. These volumes contain good, introductory treatments of distortion and magnetic tape bias signals.

Salm, W. G. 1971. *Stereo in Your Home.* Auerbach, Princeton.

Sands, Lee G., and Shunaman, F. 1969. *101 Questions and Answers about Hifi and Stereo.* Sams, Indianapolis.

Tremaine, Howard M. 1969. *Audio Cyclopedia.* Sams, Indianapolis. This massive volume is an excellent reference both for definition of terms and information about principles. Its well-written index and question-answer style are helpful.

FM

Feldman, Leonard. 1969. *FM from Antenna to Audio.* Sams, Indianapolis.

———. 1972. *FM Multiplexing for Stereo,* 3rd ed. Sams, Indianapolis. These are excellent books by a gifted author, one of the finest in the field of sound reproduction. His discussions are clear and interesting, and his illustrations are helpful. The reader is recommended to look for Feldman's several books on other topics and many periodical articles.

Tape Recording

Mee, C. D. 1964. *The Physics of Magnetic Recording.* North Holland (Interscience, N.Y.), Amsterdam. This presents a serious attempt to explain magnetic recording. It is a high level book, not for the beginner.

Nijsen, C. G. 1972. *The Tape Recorder.* Drake, New York.

Rosenthal, M. P. 1972. *Cassette and Cartridge Recorders.* Hayden, New York. This book and the one by Nijsen are appropriate for persons with no previous knowledge of tape recording. Rosenthal presents a helpful introduction to the use of the tape bias signal.

Electroacoustics; Transducers
Badmaieff, Alexis, and Davis, Don. 1966. *How to Build Speaker Enclosures.* Sams, Indianapolis. This book is now in its twelfth printing because of its popularity and usefulness. It is complete including principles and details of construction.

Cohen, A. B. 1968. *Hifi Loudspeakers and Enclosures.* Hayden, New York. For the person who wishes to build a loudspeaker system; although the book is older, its principles are applicable to a present construction of enclosures.

Fischer, F. A. 1955. *Fundamentals of Electroacoustics.* Interscience, New York.

Gayford, M. L. 1970. *Electroacoustics: Microphones, Earphones, and Loudspeakers.* Newnes-Butterworths, London. A broad survey of the topics listed in the title, this book contains an interesting and lengthy treatment of the carbon microphone.

Hunt, F. V. 1954. *Electroacoustics: The Analysis of Transduction and Its Historical Background.* Harvard Univ. Press, Cambridge.

Long, Jim. "A Microphone Primer." *Audio* 56 (12, 1972): 18; 57 (1,1973): 34. An excellent introduction to types of microphones and their various uses. Easily readable.

ELECTRONIC MUSIC
Howe, Hubert S., Jr. 1975. *Electronic Music Synthesis.* Norton, New York. Intended to be a basic textbook for electronic music courses, this book includes brief treatments of acoustics and electronic music equipment as well as the techniques of music synthesis.

Strange, Allen. 1972. *Electronic Music.* Brown, Dubuque, Ia. Although not as broad as Howe's book, this work offers a good introduction to electronic music and the techniques of synthesis.

ELECTRONICS
Brophy, James J. 1966. *Basic Electronics for Scientists.* McGraw-Hill, New York. Although the treatment of solid-state circuitry does not include recently produced devices, this text is excellent in presenting the physics of a field sometimes thought to be primarily engineering.

Hoenig, Stuart A., and Payne, F. L. 1973. *How to Build and Use Electronic Devices without Frustration, Panic, Mountains of Money, or an Engineering Degree.* Little, Brown, Boston. Highly recommended for persons who like to work with simple circuits but do not have expertise in electronics. This book teaches by doing: encouraging experimentation and construction of simple, inexpensive circuits, and explaining the principles involved. Circuits presented are useful in everyday scientific work. Note: the book presents most

topics by using op-amps (solid-state chips called operational amplifiers).

Smith, Ralph J. 1973. *Electronics: Circuits and Devices*. Wiley, New
York. Excellent text presenting physical electronics.

RCA, Solid-State Division. Latest ed. *Solid-State Devices Manual*. Somer-
ville, N.J. This book is one of a series of technical manuals produced by RCA (Motorola also produces similar material) each year.
This book contains an introduction to solid-state devices, sample
circuits for various applications, and data concerning commercially
available components.

LIST OF SYMBOLS

GREEK SYMBOLS

Δ (delta)   change in

λ (lambda)   wavelength

μ (mu)   micro

π (pi)   pi (3.14 . . .)

ρ (rho)   density

Ω (omega)   ohm

ENGLISH SYMBOLS

A amplitude; area

a acceleration

B magnetic field strength

C capacitance; compliance

c speed of light

D distance

d gap spacing

E energy

E_0 Fermi level of energy

e natural number (2.718 . . .)

F force

f frequency

g acceleration of gravity

H magnetic field

h Planck's constant; height

I intensity; current

K thermal conductivity

k spring constant

L inductance; left channel; length

l length

m mass

N number of revolutions per second

P power

p pressure

Q charge

R resistance; right channel

r radius

S speed

T temperature

t time

V voltage

v velocity

x distance; position

Z impedance

UNITS AND EQUIVALENTS

A	$(= C/s)$	ampere
C		coulomb
cm	$(= 0.01$ m$)$	centimeter
dB		decibel
F	$(= C/v)$	farad
g	$(= 0.001$ kg$)$	gram
H		henry
Hz	$(= c/s)$	hertz
in	$(= 2.54$ cm$)$	inch
J	$(= $ kg$\cdot$m$^2/$s$^2)$	joule
kg		kilogram
lb	$(= 4.4$ N$)$	pound
m		meter
N	$(= $ kg$\cdot$m$/$s$^2)$	newton
V	$(= $ J$/$C$)$	volt
W	$(= $ J$/$s$)$	watt
Ω	$(= $ V$/$A$)$	ohm

INDEX

stray, effect on magnetic tape, 97
transformer, 42, 43
Magnetic field intensity (*B*)
and cartridge output, 84
in magnetized material, 93–94
and microphone output, 35
Magnetic tape, 90–91, 96, 99–100
erasure, 97
Magnetic tape head, 89, 92–93, 97, 98
Magnetic tape recording, 89–91
audio information, 91–93, 99
bias frequency, 93–96
digital, 105–7
erasing, 97
noise, 101–2
reel-to-reel *vs.* cassette, 98–99
specifications, 163
transduction curve, 94–96
Mass, 9
and force, 10, 155–56
and kinetic energy, 157–58
and mechanical impedance, 70–71
and potential energy, 157–58
and speed of falling, 158
unit of, 16
Matrixing methods, 147–50, 152
Mechanics, topics in
acceleration, 9–11, 155–57
energy of object, 12–13, 157–58
force, 9–11, 155
Hooke's law, 11–12
position of object, 156–57
velocity of object, 115, 156
Microphone
as acoustoelectric transducer, 21, 22
choice, for recording, 33–35
damping in, 37
diaphragm motion, 12
directional response, 33–35, 144–46
distortion, 12, 35–38
frequency response, 36–38
impedance matching for, 75–76
and loudspeaker, 111
output voltage, 35–36, 42
in PA systems, 42
types of
carbon, 28–31, 38
ceramic or crystal, piezoelectric, 27–28
condenser or electrostatic (capacitor), 31–32
magnetic (dynamic), 25–27, 35–36, 111–12
moving magnet, 27
ribbon (velocity), 32–33
Modulator, 132
Monophonic reproduction. *See* Multichannel storage, retrieval
MOSFET (metal-oxide-semiconductor field-effect transistor), 54–56
Multichannel storage, retrieval
monophonic
AM radio, 132–34
digital methods, 105–7

discs, 81–86
film, 102–5
FM radio, 134–39
tape, 99–100
quadraphonic
discs, 146–50
radio, 150–53
stereophonic
discs, 86–88
FM radio, 137–39
tape, 99–100
Multiplexing, 137–39, 150–52. *See also* Multichannel storage, retrieval

Newton, 16
Newton's laws of motion, 10, 155–56
Nodes, 6, 7, 8
Noise
in AM, FM radio, 139–40
elimination, by digital methods, 105–7
signal-to-noise (S/N) ratio, 161, 162, 163
in sound system, 159
Nonlinear behavior
elimination by digital methods, 105
illustration, 12
of magnetized material, 95–96
and mechanical impedance, 36
np junction, 48–50, 51
npn transistor, 51, 52, 53, 55
n-type semiconductor, 48, 50

Ohm, 29
Ohm's law, 28–30, 74–75
Oscillation
air particles, 5
fields in radio wave, 126–29
loudspeaker diaphragm, 113–14
string, 6
Oscillator, 132, 134

Pauli exclusion principle, 46
Phase
in electrical system, 73
matching, 138
in mechanical system (driven), 68–71
in ribbon microphone, 33
of waves from loudspeaker, 118–20
Phase shifting, 151–52
Photocell, 103–4
Photons, 103–4
Pickup
electric guitar, 38
magnetic, 21
phono, 81–88, 147, 149
specifications for phono, 161
Piezoelectricity, 27
in loudspeaker, 114
in microphone, 27–28, 114
in phono cartridge, 83
Pilot tone, 138, 139, 150, 151
Planck's constant (*h*), 103–4
Plate, in vacuum tube, 43–45, 54, 103
pn junction, 48–50, 51
pnp transistor, 51